# Praise for *F.A.I.T.H.* – Volume II

"The authenticity and vulnerability of the true stories in this book are so inspiring. These women show precisely the courage it takes to move beyond your circumstances and live the life of their desires. When you open your heart and identify your dream, you too can create miracles. A must read for every woman!"

– Christy Whitman
New York Times bestselling author of *The Art of Having It All*

"I have learned in my life that the greatest gift I can ever give anyone is that they are seen and truly heard when I am with them. That's what each of the stories of *F.A.I.T.H* feels like to me: deep listening and sharing. Each of these stories is deep, insightful, and full of wisdom and heart. The writers have told their stories with such truth that it allows me as a reader to go down that path and discover what is true for me. They have lit the way for all of us to see how we are not alone and share in the joy that transformation can bring. This is a must read for anyone on a path of growth and knowledge."

– Karen Drucker, Singer/Songwriter/Author of *Let Go of the Shore*

"Open, honest, and vulnerable, the true stories within these pages drew me in. While our experiences may be different, the authors' feelings are my feelings too. They remind me that we've all been afraid, we've all made mistakes, and we all want to be loved. The discussion questions offered after each story create a space for personal awakening and healing. *F.A.I.T.H., Volume II* is a treasure for anyone who seeks to accept themselves just as they are and to know themselves at a deeper level."

– Jane Beach, author of *Choices: Choosing Me is OK* and
*How to Build a Relationship with the God of Your Understanding*

"Almost everyone has low points in life that can literally bring them to their knees. Tragically, I have several friends and know of many others who have experienced lengthy and life changing crises. I've been there too.

"In my darkest days, years ago, when 'hope' was just a four-letter word, I could have used a book exactly like this one. Each contributor has graciously authored her personal story for the betterment of others. They are not pretty or overly religious. Rather the journeys told so eloquently are raw, honest, true stories of real people in real collision courses with chaos. Somehow though, the authors climbed up and through their emotional and physical rubble, one stone at a time, as genuine survivors.

"Their experiences remind us we are not alone! We are not immune to making bad decisions or living horrific events! And we are not perfect. But we are able to use a mirror to see and accept who we really are and what we have to do to get to where we want to be!"

– Elaine C. Pereira, award-winning author of *I Will Never Forget*

"Everyone perceives obstacles in life. Some people fall victim to their challenges. Some people rise above them. Be inspired by this collection of true stories from 14 'ordinary' women who have overcome extraordinary circumstances. A must read for everyone who wants to follow their dreams!"

– Bruce D. Schneider, PhD, author of *Energy Leadership* and Founder of Institute for Professional Excellence in Coaching

"*F.A.I.T.H. – Finding Answers in the Heart, Volume II* is a magnificent book. This compilation of true stories and personal prompts for the readers invites deep exploration and inspires creativity and transformation. As Director of the Bay Area Critical Incident Stress Management Team and founding member of the Center for Living with Dying program (now of Bill Wilson Center), I have been present for responders and citizens facing the most critical of incidents and the most heartrending grief for almost 40 years. This amazing book is a guide to map the journey of healing on the road to survival in building the new normal. I am ever grateful for the courage of the authors and its timely message."

– Janet Childs, MA, AAETS Diplomate, Director, Bay Area CISM Team
Director of Training, Education and Crisis Intervention
Centre for Living with Dying program of Bill Wilson Center

"*Finding Answers in the Heart* is a collection of candid stories of ordinary women who have transcended varied forms of pain, violence, and grief to help themselves and others get to a place of peace and healing. Sharing their journey from fear and doubt to triumph and strength reveals a powerful recipe for others who are struggling with their own vulnerabilities. These amazing women affirm that you can—and must—find your worth and purpose so that you stay grounded in spite of the troubled and chaotic world around you. Truly inspiring!

– Jamala Rogers, Author, Columnist for *The St. Louis American*

"Every now and then a book comes along that has it all. It's inspiring, easy to read, true to life, and heart-warming. That's *F.A.I.T.H. Finding Answers in the Heart, Volume II*. The stories are poignant and powerful and filled with the promise of assisting the reader in finding the gems within to jumpstart her life.

"Grace and ease are two words that so resonate for me, and two qualities I desire to create more of in my life, and I've found this book to deliver both for me personally. Inspiration abounds and I highly recommend you read the wisdom contained within this book."

– Marti Murphy, Master Abundance Coach
Founder and CEO of Wisdom International Institute, Inc.

"I feel honored to have experienced one of the first looks inside this warm and thought-provoking series of experiences and interactions by this group of amazing women who actually brought their individual journeys to life for the reader. Some might think that this compilation of hope, strength, and victory is designed for women readers alone. But that is far from the truth. As a man, I walked some of these roads through the authors' words, positioned to feel their pain, guilt, shame, and joy.

"They enabled you to not only see what they saw, but by some inner spiritual power of existence, they take your hand and walk you through feeling what they felt. It would be hard and unfair to pick out one particular journey taken by these women and use it as a focal point for all the rest, simply because each journey is a masterpiece in itself. I call it a masterpiece because their experiences were painted onto a mental canvas that will stay with the reader forever. I applaud these authors, and hold them up as ministers to a hurting population."

– Eddie L. Speaks
Author and TV show host and producer, Atlanta's 57 WATC

"It was an honor to experience reading this book. The sheer vulnerability displayed showed these courageous women baring their souls. The stories weave a beautiful tapestry of journeys to healing that are written in such a grounded way that I can't imagine them not resonating with people. The power to affect change is palpable in this book, and it is a catalyst for self-reflection and self-exploration."

– Ericka Goodwin, MD
Board-certified child, adolescent, and adult psychiatrist

"The dyslexic in me thought that I would only read one chapter of the book; however, that one chapter became such an easy read that I was drawn and pulled into reading more. I read the book probably the fastest I have ever read any book in my entire life. It shows you the power of sharing our stories and to know that our stories have value. It's wonderful to see yourself in people and realize that you really are not alone in your struggles and your journey. It reminded me how we are so connected and it felt very inspiring.

– Wendy Battaglia
Horticultural therapist, artist, and program manager at ZFusion, Inc.

"If you want honesty, this is it. *F.A.I.T.H. Volume II* speaks in plain language—true language—straight from the real experiences of fourteen women telling their stories. Each author presents the unwrapped and unedited version of her mistakes, her blindnesses, her stumbling blocks. And each has clearly learned and evolved. That's the strength of each story, and of the book—not WHAT happened to each, but that SOME-THING happened, and each one got through it. They're better for it. Each of us has that same potential, and it starts with having faith in oneself."

– Ann Voorhees Baker, Founder and Producer of Women At Woodstock

"We all go through dark moments in life. The stories of the women in this book show how we can move through our tribulations to eventually triumph in the face of challenge. I am inspired by the courage and persistence of these women. You may find a piece of yourself in each woman's story."

– Françoise Everett
Divine Living Certified Coach for Women Entrepreneurs

# F.A.I.T.H.

### Finding Answers in the Heart™

## Volume II

*To my mother,*

*May you always remember to listen to the still small voice within!*

*Love,*
*Ricia*
*4/30/15*

# F.A.I.T.H.

Finding Answers in the Heart™

## Volume II

Azizi Blissett • Terry Crump • Linda Goodman • Suzanne Baker Hogan
Barbara J. Hopkinson • Judy Keating • Rebecca Kirson
Nanette Littlestone • Ricia L. Maxie • Corinna Murray • Lynn Rekvig
Lorelei Robbins • Angela Rodriguez • Maureen Roe

WORDS OF PASSION • ATLANTA

F.A.I.T.H. – Finding Answers in the Heart, Volume II

Published by Words of Passion, Atlanta, GA 30097.

Book Production: Nanette Littlestone
Editorial: Nanette Littlestone
Cover and Interior Design:
    Nanette Littlestone and Peter Hildebrandt

To receive a free e-mail newsletter delivering inspirational tips and updates about *F.A.I.T.H.*, register directly at http://www.FindingAnswersInTheHeart.com.

ISBN: 978-0-9960709-2-8

Dedicated to those who
wish to move through life with
ease, grace, and gratitude.
May you always
have F.A.I.T.H.

# Contents

If you aren't good at loving yourself, you will have a difficult time loving anyone, since you'll resent the time and energy you give another person that you aren't even giving to yourself.

– Barbara De Angelis

Nanette Littlestone

# Lost and Found

*You'll meet someone who wants to take care of you. It would be okay to be pampered. It would be okay to be babied. And it would be okay to be with someone whose idea of 'take your breath away' is lamination. Sealing you in a bubble so you don't get exposed to anyone else's potential relationship germs so that you're guaranteed to stay with him. . . . You'll hit a point in the relationship where you'll peak out in terms of the quality that you're getting, level off for a while, and then start to drop. When you start to drop down, that's your bailout time. If you're really fast, it's 9 months. If you're really slow, it could be 3 years.*
— Astrology reading, March 1989

The islands were calling me. Tropical breezes and soft white sand and aquamarine water so clear you could count the indentations in the seashells. So what was I doing in Bakersfield, California where the summer heat baked your brains and the winter fog made driving a terror?

3

Good question.

I'd moved from Los Angeles for the opportunity to manage the one-man office of a family law attorney. But after three years of crazy growth and 12-hour days my effervescence had fizzed out. I was tired of the job, tired of the fixed salary, and tired of the scenery. I wanted a change. Somewhere nicer, different, and far away from there. Somewhere tropical.

One cold winter night my boss walked me to my car in the deserted parking lot. I scraped ice off my windshield and said, "I'm thinking about moving to Hawaii."

"So why don't you?" he asked.

I realized I'd been waiting for permission. All those months of wishing and wanting and hoping and telling myself I wasn't sure, and all I could think was *Why not?* There were no ties holding me, no family, no dependents. I could do what I wanted. So in April of 1989 I quit my job, packed my bags, shipped my car, and moved to Kihei in southwest Maui.

Paradise was wonderful—the ocean, the long stretches of pristine sand, the greenery, the enormous, glorious flowers. This was what I'd been waiting for. My soul expanded and I breathed deeper. But was it expensive! I found a clerical job (way below my skill level), a decent apartment, bought the cheapest food I could find, and settled into a routine. Not exactly the stuff of my dreams, but living right across the street from the ocean and walking along the beach filled my soul with little glimmers of satisfaction. I was doing okay.

Then in June I met *him*.

I was walking on the beach in the morning sun, trailing my feet in the water and minding my business. I loved my walks, how my feet sank in the sand, the repetitive heel/ toe that stretches the muscles and relaxes the mind. Just me and the ocean and the energy of the water. I finished my usual half-mile and turned to come back. I was feeling good, refreshed, and there he was. Fifty yards away, his body tanned and strong, sitting on the sand in lotus position like a sun god. Self-conscious now, I walked until I was almost parallel with his position and, flustered, I turned to the sea. Seconds later, a wave washed around my feet and a seashell tumbled in the receding water. I dipped in my hand and pulled out a slender conical shell. As I held it in my palm, something dark brown extruded from the shell. I'd never held a live shell before. Surely this was a sign of something important.

"You must have magic," he said. His name was Greg. Heat emanated from him as he stood next to me, several inches taller. His blond hair gleamed in the sun and his blue eyes sparkled. We walked down the beach where I released the living shell and talked about metaphysics and menehunes— Hawaiian fairies. His words ran together in quick succession and washed over me in a haze. I understood very little and it didn't matter. I was mesmerized. This was what I'd been waiting for.

In less than an hour we were driving my car down the coast to Hana, a three-hour trip along winding roads through spectacular scenery. My stomach pitched with each hairpin turn. We took a break about halfway in and I rested on the trunk of the car while Greg wandered down the road. When he came back I smelled cigarettes on his breath. I hate smoking and told him in no uncertain terms that if he wanted to be with me he wouldn't smoke. "I want to be with you," he said. "I love you."

Love me? He just met me. But he threw away his cigarettes and we drove on. We had sandwiches from a roadside vendor, perused the shops, and lay out in the sun at a park. I asked Greg to tell me when my skin started to turn pink. I burn easily. Two hours later I woke up from a nap and my skin was red and hot. Greg was still asleep.

Sleezy lines. Not keeping his word. Not caring about my well-being. What kind of man had I hooked up with?

He apologized profusely for his neglect. We got back to my apartment very late and he told me he had nowhere to sleep. Despite the earlier warning signs, the eternal nurturer in me oozed empathy. I let him crash on the couch.

My mid-30s had already arrived and I'd never lived with someone. How would I know how it felt if I didn't try it? He moved in the next day.

Greg drove me to work in the morning, left me with dreamy kisses, and picked me up in the afternoon. He treated me to nice dinners now and then, cooked for me, drove me to the top of Mt. Haleakala for the sunrise, and showered me with attention. Tale after tale he spun of top secret government jobs, living overseas, being friends with celebrities. I wanted adventure and this was it. There were stirrings of unease as well. He didn't seem to have a real job, and I never met any friends. But money appeared not to be an issue so I pushed the unease aside.

In July he mentioned the Pacific Northwest and we decided to go. Just like that. I loved Maui and couldn't really afford it, and I had never seen the Pacific Northwest. So many times with new boyfriends I had woven fantasies about traveling only to have them deflate in disappointment. Here was my chance. If I didn't go now, when would I? Once again, I quit my job, packed my bags—*we* packed *our* bags—shipped my car, and left paradise.

Travel on the road was idyllic. I lounged in the passenger seat and absorbed the marvels. We drove from Seattle across the Canadian border. Summer in the Rockies took my breath away and the scenery was enhanced by Greg's audacious spirit. Many times we parked the car and hiked along trails to investigate the plant life, waterfalls, just sit on a rock and catch the sun's rays. We had all the time in the world and no agenda. It was bliss. We celebrated my birthday in Penticton on the lake where I drove a jet ski for the first time and had a blast. Then we headed south through Spokane to Moscow, Idaho where I had amazing roast beef at a nondescript diner, through the acrid odor of the paper mills in Lewiston, and onto the beautiful lakefront property of McCall where we talked about buying land.

But the wonders of the trip were overbalanced by the harsh realities of finances and behaviors. He took charge; I enabled. We had no money to speak of; we were living off my credit cards. Six of them. Gas, hotels, food, all the conveniences of travel were paid for by me and I worried about the increasing debt. But how did I stop now? I loved him. I wanted to be with him. Where else could I go? What else would I do?

I vaguely remembered the independent woman who moved to Hawaii on her own to stake her claim. Vaguely.

Greg's liquor consumption increased. By the time we reached Boise, we'd been on the road for two months and the wandering life tried my emotions. I plotted in my head about leaving, I complained and withdrew, I argued with him about his drinking. He reasoned with me. "Everybody drinks a little" or "A lot of research shows that alcohol is therapeutic." And I gave in.

The alcohol may have been therapeutic but our rising expenses were not. One week later I broke down. I needed stability, I needed a rest, I needed someone I could trust to take care of me. I wanted my mother. He drove me to the airport, I charged the ticket to Los Angeles to my one remaining credit card, and I left him in Idaho with my car. I loved my car, but my sanity was more important.

Over the next few weeks I recuperated, mentally and physically. I might have recovered emotionally, but he called me every night, and his voice pulled at my heart. By the time he arrived at my parent's house with my car—he brought it back!—I was attached to him once again.

Next stop—just four months after we met—Arizona.

October in Phoenix. The temperatures were warm, not hot, and the desert offered a fascinating array of cacti. But the dry, dusty air left me choking and coughing and I developed horrible allergies. I found a job as a receptionist in a landscape architecture firm in Scottsdale. He bought used cars, fixed them up, and sold them. Unfortunately, the only cars he (we) could afford were on their last legs, and the "fixes" added nothing to the value, so we continued to lose money on the sales. My income was all that kept us housed and fed.

By November I developed a bronchial condition and couldn't afford to see a doctor. We drove to Los Angeles to see my parents for Thanksgiving and the trip was brutal. I thought I would cough up a lung. Three months later, my health improved, but my car payments were in arrears. The collectors began to call with distressing lectures and threats of doom that made my heart pound in fear. Could they really garnish my wages? I asked Greg for help and he said they're just harassing you, it doesn't mean anything.

Then one day the car was gone.

Shortly after that I filed for bankruptcy. Resentment curled under my skin and festered. We could have found a way out of our debt, I was sure of it. All we needed was a plan. Why couldn't he have helped? I wanted to shout at him, to scream about injustice, but I held my emotions inside. I didn't know how to speak up.

The following year in June, just before the summer heat, we left Arizona in one of our fixer-upper cars and headed back to the Northwest, ending up in Portland, Oregon. Portland in the summer is glorious with its majestic pines and snowy peaks. I fell in love with Mt. Hood, the deep blues of glacial lakes, amazing food, and the casual attitude of downtown commerce. I worked as a Customer Service Rep for Pacific Telecom and handled accounts for Canada. And loved it! Greg bought and sold cars—again. My salary, this time, far exceeded what I was making in Arizona so we lived comfortably in a nice 2-bedroom apartment. Yet every month a huge portion of my paycheck made its way into his pocket for car repairs and we had very little for nice meals or fun.

Time cycled through the holidays—Christmas, Valentine's Day, my birthday, his birthday. We explored hiking trails in the summer and sledded on the slopes of Mt. Hood in the winter. But as we moved into the third year of our relationship the luster decayed and antagonism built. His drinking picked up and he gained a lot of weight. He swore he wasn't smoking but I smelled cigarettes. Watching him guzzle a liter of beer every night in front of the TV ignited my irritation. His habits tore at the weak strands of emotional fiber that kept me from going insane. When I found one of my prize knives lying in water in the sink, something I had repeatedly told him not to do, I wanted to plunge the knife into his pillow and rip it to shreds.

Work provided a sanctuary, the place where I felt connected and safe. If only I could have stayed there at night. At home, anger brewed and created tension. Whatever attraction I'd held for him vanished, and I longed to be on my own. Each night when I lay next to him the voice in my head said *Let me out, let me out.* But I didn't know how to leave. I had no money for another apartment. Where would I live? What would happen to my belongings?

The need to end the relationship spiraled and I started to weigh his words. "You're prettier than she is," he would tell me while a gorgeous model danced on TV and I would compare myself to her and know he was lying. "I love you" he would say while he drank yet another beer and wanted to have sex. They were lies, all lies, as were his staying out late and the smell of cigarettes on his breath. Distrust and revulsion roared.

The gradual descent into emotional hell gave me a strong foundation. One night I'd simply had enough. While he was working on a car, somewhere, I called a friend and asked if I could stay with her the next night, packed a duffle bag, and stashed it in the closet. The following day I got up early, left a note on the kitchen counter, grabbed my bag, and went to work. I trembled the whole time, hoping he wouldn't call, dreading the call, waiting for him to call and scream at me, wondering why he hadn't called.

Then he called.

His voice was soft and gentle. "You can come home. You don't have to worry. I won't do anything."

I started to cry. I hadn't expected him to be nice.

"I'm packing my bags," he said, "and I'll be ready to leave when you get here. It's okay. You can come home."

"Okay," I whispered, then I put my head on my arms and sobbed.

When I got home I saw his bags by the door. He smiled at me, tenderly, and held out his arms. We hugged for a long time and my tears wet his shirt. He was remarkably calm. I was drained and sad. Then he kissed me goodbye and walked out the door.

I cried the rest of the night.

The next day I sent my mother a letter to tell her I had ended the relationship with Greg and I asked her not to call me. I wasn't ready to talk.

When I called, her first words were, "Are you alright?" I said yes and she said, "I'm so glad you're not with him anymore. I never liked him." Leave it to my mom to make me laugh.

My next paycheck offered a huge surprise. With Greg gone, I no longer had to fork over hundreds of dollars for car repairs and parts purchases. All of my money stayed with me. I was stunned to discover that I had an extra $750 per month. Lovely!

Several months later I also discovered that he'd left me with the generous gift of herpes. Lovely!

My astrologer was right. The relationship lasted three years. I was pretty slow at letting go. It took another two years and four relationships for me to get over the indiscretions of my past and *find* myself. When I did, though, I found something else—the love of my life. My astrologer was right about that too. He said "you'll find your ultimate [love] in 1994." I met my husband at a house party that summer. The timing wasn't quite right then; we had a bit of juggling to do before we could settle down. But we eventually did and we've been married 16 years now, 16 amazing years. He appreciates me, believes in me, and supports me and I do the same for him. That's the way true love works.

Every lesson contains a gift. I willingly embarked on that adventure because I had soul lessons to learn. Lessons in self-confidence, self-esteem, self-worth, and, most importantly, self-love. I allowed someone else to control my life and make decisions for me. I gave up my power, the power that stems from knowing who I am. Falling in love is euphoric, and wonderful. What can compare to that bliss? But sacrificing my Self in the process showed a lack of self-love. It took me three years to pay attention to those intuitive nudges, the ones that said something was wrong. When I did I found the strength to change my course. I found the strength to start loving myself again.

I got lost on my journey with Greg. You may too. Everybody makes mistakes in life. But just because you were once lost doesn't mean you can't be found. Let faith guide you. If you follow your heart and listen to its messages, you'll find your way to peace, self-confidence, and more joy than you can imagine.

## Discussion Questions

1. Where have you been lost in life (with a job, relationship, financial situation, etc.)? What were the circumstances around that experience?
2. If you could go through that experience again, what would you change, and why?
3. What lesson did that experience teach you?
4. What was the gift in that lesson? How did that make you stronger or more loving?

*Nanette Littlestone, owner of Words of Passion, works with inspirational authors to overcome writers block, master correct grammar, create strong structure, and write with clarity and passion. She specializes in helping women write from the heart so they can put their passion into words and inspire others. www.wordsofpassion.com*

You were put on this earth to achieve your greatest self, to live out your purpose, and to do it courageously.

— Steve Maraboli

# Awakening to Truth

Our journeys ebb and flow like the movement of water as it cascades down a bed of stone, searching for the next crevice to fill or rock to glide over as it navigates finding a pool to rest in a Zen-like state. The unfolding of our lives can be as simple as that grace. Yet our journeys often seem filled with holes where the water collects, stagnating at times, or diverting where a boulder has split the stream, directing the water much differently than originally intended. At the time we may curse the diversions, not truly understanding that the new path is actually a much needed realignment because living the unconscious life will never get us to a full expression of our purpose and gifts. On the unconscious path we don't even know our purpose. We navigate life as a series of events to react to versus actively creating the life we desire. We "happen" into our circumstances and complain because it always feels lacking and how can it not when we play the role of victim? And we feel the void inside of our hearts and souls. The void that tells us there is much more to life than we are aware of and much more to this universe than we have any clue. *And then it happens . . . a life event so profound that we are given pause, shaken in such a way that we can't help but Awaken to our Truth.*

Aiden Grace Lafferty was born on June 24, 2002. After a trip to San Francisco with family, I noticed that I felt dehydrated and sensed that something was off. I had a routine visit scheduled shortly after with my physician and she confirmed my suspicions. My amniotic fluid levels were dangerously low and infection had set in. Despite my being ordered to bed rest by my doctor for a week-long hospital stay, the magnesium sulfate was not effective in stopping the contractions. Aiden came into this world prematurely at 27 weeks and weighed two pounds two ounces. She spent shy of two weeks on the Neonatal Intensive Care Unit (NICU). All reports from the Neonatologist were good regarding the core issues preemies typically have with stomach, lung, and brain development. We thought we were in the clear. But "the clear" doesn't always factor in course diversions like gram negative bacteria. I received the call Friday afternoon from the doctor. "Aiden has taken a turn for the worse. Get here as soon as you can. We don't know how long she has." They tried to insert a line in her tiny little wrist as a last-ditch effort to give her more oxygen. Her body was filling up with too much carbon dioxide. She had been exposed to the hospital borne infection *Pseudomonas* which results in sepsis and shortly thereafter, death. Aiden Grace Lafferty left this world less than two weeks after her arrival. She died on July 6, 2002.

I was *Completely. Thrown. Off. Course.* I had prepared myself for being a mother. Prior to finding out that I was pregnant, I was on the career track. I worked as a Business Manager at my husband's family business, a software development company. We were in our late 20s and didn't put much thought into the direction of our lives aside from taking the next step: graduating college, getting married, having a child, establishing a career. Wash, rinse, repeat; walk the path that has been laid down like so many who have come before you. Follow the herd to arrive at the mystical "American Dream." Except the American Dream didn't make allowances for tragedy and we had just suffered one. So I did what any self-respecting young person does who doesn't have the awareness or emotional wherewithal to deal with the profound grief she had just experienced. I immediately went back to work, applied for graduate school, and began an intense Executive MBA program two months later.

Everyone has their response to pain. My drug of choice was to work harder. If you stay two steps ahead of feeling the emotion, then you don't have to! Immersing myself fully in a left-brained activity seemed like the perfect answer to an imperfect course diversion. I had no idea that the Executive program had a HUGE emphasis on personal development and right-brained exploration or that I would come out of the 18-month program a completely changed person. Still not awakened to my truth, but completely changed, nonetheless. With a renewed confidence in myself and a lot of insight garnered from an array of personality assessments and leadership inventories, I decided it was time to embark on the journey of entrepreneurship in a business with my brother.

We partnered together for five beautiful years masterfully creating ponds and waterfalls. Living works of art in our clients' backyards. It was an adventure but one that would come to an end when the housing market crashed and I felt I could no longer leverage my future to support the company's payroll. The work was transformational in nature but it was my brother's passion more than mine. I had once again put off finding my calling to facilitate the dreams of someone else. My life was not "business as usual" and I felt the closing of many chapters coming to a head simultaneously. I closed IrisBlade Pond & Patio and ended a nine-year marriage. The decision to leave my marriage was one I had wrestled with for five years. Lacking courage, I chose sameness and stability over honoring my truth. My husband was one of the kindest souls I had ever met, however we were on very different paths of growth and our relationship had withered over time until we became roommates at best.

A year and a half after my divorce, I took a trip to San Francisco with a man I was dating who attended a conference. San Francisco would once again color my life. I had reconnected with an old friend who, ironically, I had parted ways with after Aiden's death in order to facilitate growth for both of us. She was so moved by the loss that she went into a nursing program and worked in the NICU at Stanford. I hadn't seen her in eight years. I also hadn't met her husband or two young children. They picked me up and we found a pizzeria for lunch. This lunch would forever alter the course of my life and I was no stranger to transition and change. I didn't know a lot about Marika's current life or her husband, Peter. I didn't know Peter had a near death experience that was a course diversion for him resulting in mediumship abilities. Nor did I know the next three hours would be filled with messages from beyond as Peter shared communication from Aiden and two of my uncles who had passed. Aiden's message was simple. "Wake up. Stop living small. Stop blaming yourself for my death. Stop repeating the same patterns in your jobs and relationships while you live from your ego and fear. Leave the job that you hate and the relationships that don't treat you with love and respect because *you* don't treat you with love and respect. Discover your true purpose as a healer and live it with passion!" I received the information through solid tears and heavy feelings.

I devoted the next few years to "discovering my true purpose." I started to open to the notion of "spirituality" and the connection to Source. I began studying spirituality and metaphysics. Through a daily OM email message, I found my way to the Akashic Records. I invested with a teacher who taught me how to work with my intuition to access the Records, also referred to as the "Book of Life." The Records are a repository for all of our thoughts, feelings, intentions, and deeds of every lifetime ever lived back to our moment of origination from Source/God/the Universe.

I worked on increasing my conscious awareness and began powerfully shifting all aspects of my life to live from a place of love versus fear. I created the shifts by connecting in with profound Akashic wisdom combined with energy clearing which resulted in Soul level healing. In the records, I discovered *my sacred truth*: my soul's purpose, my life lessons, soul level gifts, and the blocks and restrictions that resulted from past choices I had made that I continued to play out in this life. I reclaimed my power in the places where I had unknowingly given it away by identifying the energy anchors and energy drains. I released the people who were no longer aligned to the path I wanted to walk. I took responsibility for all that had happened before. With Aiden's inspiration, I committed to healing the wounds around feeling like I was never enough, not feeling safe and supported, and a lack of self-love that I had carried most of my life, wounds that kept me repeating patterns, making excuses, and hiding my light.

As the spiritual master Lao Tzu quoted, "Water is the softest thing, yet it can penetrate mountains and earth. This shows clearly the principle of softness overcoming hardness." Aiden brought me many gifts during the short time she was with me. Most importantly, I awoke to the truth that the power to change my life had always existed within me. I was the soft flowing force that could penetrate the fixed and un-yielding obstacles I encountered on my journey. Ultimately in life, when we can let go of our sorrow and pain to bring in a higher level of awareness and understanding, we can see that a different vantage point offers us wholeness and healing. Connecting with faith and trusting in the process *can* lead us to greater levels of insight, wisdom, and soul level healing.

## Discussion Questions

1. How does the metaphor of water apply to your life? Where are you searching?

2. When have you been thrown off course? How did you respond to that "diversion"? Was that the right path for you? What would you do differently now?

3. Have you found your true purpose? If not, what blocks and restrictions are in the way? Where are you willing to release and forgive? Where can you shift from fear to love?

*Rebecca Kirson is a transformational coach committed to raising her clients' levels of awareness so they can live in alignment with their Soul's Purpose. With her intuitive insight her clients create a life of abundance, purpose, and power. Rebecca has an Executive MBA, plus a background in Psychology, Human Development, and Family Studies. www.yoursacredtruth.com*

. . . and when one of them meets the other half, the actual half of himself, whether he be a lover of youth or a lover of another sort, the pair are lost in an amazement of love and friendship and intimacy and one will not be out of the other's sight, as I may say, even for a moment . . .

— Plato

# Bliss is Free

I am flying towards England, meeting the morning light. I am speeding towards a man I have never met in person, but in my heart, I have known him forever. Back home, I have left my domestic world in ruins. And somehow, I feel completely free.

Never in a million years did I think I would be on this plane. Never did I guess that I would turn my beautiful life upside down. The last thing I wanted was to hurt my family. But at forty-three, the other half of my soul came calling. And though it might seem selfish, I had no choice but to answer. When I did, I found myself.

*My heart knew the way. It called my human self to love. When I did, I touched the stars.*

My story is a love story. It might sound unbelievable, but it is true. I was missing half of my soul, and he found me in this life. He woke me up when I least expected it and revived me with infinite love. From that moment on, everything changed.

*This challenge that I never saw coming had the power to shake me up and deliver invaluable riches.*

My marriage had been beautiful. My husband was such a compassionate, attractive, and peaceful man. We were sweet partners for two decades and extremely faithful spouses. I never had a thought about anyone else. We logged all-nighters on a regular basis, taking care of our children's health. Three hospital stays later, we kept creating a grateful and beautiful life.

My husband and I shared so much love for a very long time. We gave everything we had, but we were opposites. And inevitably, opposites go to their corners and live in separate rooms.

My husband did not engage with me emotionally, and my soul craved that connection. I longed for a togetherness we'd never had. Spirituality separated us further. As I grew to see a larger reality, he did not support my beliefs or my work. This created a whole new divide.

It became clear that we were not going to grow old understanding each other. We had pledged to different kingdoms on alien shores. Our life would have slipped quietly into the sea like a pink sun at some overpriced resort. And we would have said that we were lucky. But fate intervened.

*Following my heart was about finding myself. It was finally honoring the dreams I had tucked away and given up on. And it took a crisis to remember them.*

Crisis came in the form of another man. We met through our spiritual blogs, half a world away. We corresponded for two months in pure innocence and became supportive friends. This was one of many spiritual connections I talked openly about. I didn't even know what this person looked like, but I was starting to care about him like family.

Then one day, without warning, my heart blew wide open in my chest. The physical sensation was overpowering, and it came out of nowhere while I was driving. I had to pull the car over and sit in disbelief. "What is happening to me?" I gasped. "I am falling in love with Spencer. And there is nothing I can do to stop it." It was April Fool's Day, the day I remembered my other half.

In the past, I had been blessed to know romantic love. I had a high school boyfriend who was Romeo to my Juliet. Years later, I fell in love with my husband and saw fireworks that crackled with destiny. But this new love was spiritual resurrection, the resurrection of myself.

Ecstasy poured in from four thousand miles away and ignited my entire being. Unconditional love I'd only read about became mine to experience. I realized that all the love I'd known before had been conditional, no matter how earthly beautiful and sweet. This love was purely infinite and all-accepting. This was how life was supposed to be! I felt like a spiritual rock star.

*I was awakening to my soul. I was remembering the love I had always been.*

So here I was, shocked to find myself in this situation, and I was bombarded by challenges galore. But love overruled them all. This man wasn't "perfect" by human standards, yet I felt how immaculate his being was. As absurd as it sounds, we both knew that we'd loved each other for eons, well before this life. We had been kept apart for lifetimes. The longing was unbearable. And still we hadn't met.

I felt horrible for having these feelings in my marriage. That week, I shared the truth openly with my husband, with complete honesty. The whole experience was extremely painful, and we started going to counseling.

Next, I told my friends, my sister, and parents what was going on. It was the only way that I could honor everyone affected. Or so I thought.

I endured no end of judgment from my family, and who could blame them? How could anyone understand the power of this love that threatened our life? It felt impossible to explain that I *had* to be with this person, that I felt such pain from being apart. This love was more real than my beating heart, but it was like defending God to atheists. And I had to bear the task.

People saw it as your standard affair, even though I hadn't physically had one. I was a cheater who couldn't help herself, and what's worse, I was taking everyone along for the ride. I was asking them to understand why I was smashing up our beautiful life.

It didn't help that I'd seemed so content all those years, that somehow I had promised I would always be happily married with a beautiful family in a storybook house. And though I might sound ungrateful, I felt trapped in convention. People were shocked when I wanted out.

*Freedom had slipped away little by little. It was stolen, bit by bit, until one day I realized that I had been the thief. I had been robbing myself of my dreams and justifying the burglary to everyone. I had defended why I didn't need what made my heart beat.*

Few understood my liberation. Most tried to listen, but I was treated like a fool. My family wondered, "Why can't she just stay put? How could she do this to her children, and to us?" They told me they were worried about my safety and security. I worried they didn't know love like this.

I was challenging their entire world, and even though we live in modern times, they tried their best to stop me. They resorted to shame and threatened my rights. I was interrogated like a child and ostracized for being honest. I was ridiculed for my spiritual beliefs. But what surprised me most was how severely I judged myself.

At some point, I realized that I was punishing myself more than anyone. I felt so guilty for hurting people that I swam in judgment for over a year. I put my spiritual writing on hold as well as my new relationship. I started slinking away from my rights like a pariah, as though I was asking to be penalized for following my heart.

The whole ordeal begged me to finally love myself. I was being challenged to own my worth and take my rightful place in life. And so I began to purge the guilt that riddled me and give myself unconditional love. In fact, I started feeling unconditional love for everyone who'd reflected my turmoil back. I learned total, spiritual acceptance, and I saw that I don't have to earn my dreams. I already deserve them.

*Resisting bliss was hard and expensive, and I'd paid dearly through my lack of self-worth. My bliss didn't require a debilitating price. It was always meant to be free.*

Like many women, I had been trained to be a pleaser who didn't want too much. Conservative society had encouraged me to become a wife and to feel damn lucky that I was privileged. Comfortable moms aren't supposed to wake up.

Well, I did, but with deep soul love for my husband. Throughout our crisis, I prayed that he would experience resurrection of his own. I knew that our time together was precious, as were the lessons we were teaching each other. And though I hated hurting him, I knew that this situation was intended by our souls. Somehow, throughout our divorce, we maintained a loving atmosphere for our children.

I lived apart from my Beloved, and the odds weren't in my favor to permanently unite. You see, true love is entwined with tragedy for good reason. Because the power of a soul coming back together is such an intensely painful process that separation can seem easier. Harmony only happens when both people have healed enough to love themselves.

And when they do, they elevate the entire planet. They light up our world with unconditional love. Imagine how helpful this is during these changing times for humanity. The real purpose of true love is astounding.

*All the great love songs are true. There is a perfect other half of your soul. Perhaps this person is on earth right now, and they will show you how to finally love yourself. Even if you aren't together, this is what you will learn the most.*

My love story didn't end tragically. Despite overwhelming challenges, Spencer and I are growing closer towards each other every day. We've kept a faith as mighty as the ocean between us, and have never stopped following our hearts. We were pushed to grow exponentially, and we are awestruck by the love that we hold.

I learned that what I've been through is called a "Twin Flame" experience, and I want to help others who face this challenge too. By writing about my story and sharing what I know, I have found sublime purpose. I want everyone to know such fulfillment because it is attainable if you follow your heart.

So if you find yourself justifying why you don't have what you want—I don't mean possessions, but purpose, self-love, the independence to be authentic, the partnership you crave, and friends who really get and support you—then stop settling right now. Stop limiting what is yours to have, no matter how scary that might seem. Go for your dreams! The bliss that you deserve is real. And you don't have to pay any price.

## Discussion Questions

1. When have you experienced an unforeseen challenge? What were your thoughts and emotions? What were the thoughts and emotions of the people around you?

2. How often do you judge others? How does that judgment reflect your feelings and beliefs?

3. What is your definition of love and self-love? How does that affect your relationships?

4. Where do you resist your bliss? Where are you not honoring your dreams?

*Suzanne Baker Hogan is a spiritual writer. She is the author of SharetheSpiritual.com, a metaphysical blog designed to guide you through humanity's spiritual evolution. Suzanne is here to help you actualize your fullest human potential during these extraordinary times. www.sharethespiritual.com*

Something amazing happens when we surrender and just love. We melt into another world, a realm of power already within us. The world changes when we change. The world softens when we soften. The world loves us when we choose to love the world.

— Marianne Williamson

CORINNA MURRAY
# Embracing Surrender

Finding my way through life, I began to notice that all of my memorable experiences had been marked by emotion. All of my greatest challenges were powerfully, emotionally charged, and because of the discomfort in experiencing those feelings, I was led to seek emotional relief. My emotions determined the actions I took and directed the choices I made in any given moment in order to consciously, or unconsciously, feel better. It sounds so simple but it is incredibly profound to me. It is the *why* of who I am and why I am compelled to share my story with you.

The catalyst to my awakening came in the form of breast cancer. I was 51, a veterinarian by profession, a mother of three, one of whom was born severely disabled, and in a long-term and committed marriage. On the evening of November 11, 2010, my youngest son probably saved my life. He was stoically recovering from a painful procedure to correct a malformed ribcage. While probing his ribs he asked me what normal ribs felt like. I started to feel my upper ribs. To my surprise, which quickly turned to horror, I found a large mass at the top of my left breast. I had not had a mammogram in almost three years. Not only was it time-consuming and uncomfortable, I arrogantly believed I was immune to cancer. I had been a vegetarian for years, a daily exercise addict, and had no family history of cancer. I was quickly and profoundly humbled the next day when my fears were confirmed by my doctors.

In my initial stages of fear, panic, and confusion, I could not think. I needed help figuring out my next steps. I needed to know that my family would be okay, even if I died. I wanted to blame someone (me) or something (environmental toxins/hormones/radiation, etc.) I wanted knowledgeable guidance and relief from uncertainty. Gratefully, I embraced the wonderful doctors and nurses who initially worked with me. I followed their lead, like a deer in headlights, and scheduled a radical double mastectomy and reconstruction with the first plastic surgeon I consulted.

But this storm was bigger than my cancer. My father-in-law passed away on the day I had a diagnostic biopsy, then my mother broke her hip just days before I was scheduled for surgery. As awful as it sounds, their timing was divine. It forced me to step out of my drama and really look at these life and death events to gain clarity about what really mattered. For most of my life, I ignored that feeling inside of me that knew there was a better way. I always just tried to plow through and get things done as I pushed away pesky feelings of dis-ease, insisting on struggling through life. But something was different about NOW. I started to understand that all I could really do well was to be fully present and surrender to what was at hand from an emotional place of forgiveness, compassion, and acceptance. I forgave my father-in law for dying when I needed my husband's attention. I forgave my husband's unavailability and felt compassion for his loss. I forgave my mother for trumping me when I was in crisis and compassionately accepted her need for my help. I accepted my cancer and forgave myself for being its victim. I felt better, more centered, but it was not easy. I still wanted the cancer out of me NOW and did not want to waste precious time.

So I stopped. I stopped to cry, to breathe, and then to look at this "divine intervention" as a sign to find another plan, a plan where I could manage my family dramas while more fully focusing on all of my treatment options. At first, I did not have much support. My husband had to deal with his loss and help his mother. A few close friends lovingly gave me comfort, but this was really my journey. I kept the cancer secret from my kids for weeks until I had a plan. I tried to be normal for them. I also started to pay more attention to my emotions, my divine guidance.

Soon thereafter, I consulted with oncologists. They told me "It's not the tumor in your breast that will kill you; it's the cells that get away that will." That hit me hard because Elizabeth Edwards was in the news daily as she succumbed to her metastatic breast cancer. So I decided to go with chemotherapy prior to surgery to shrink the tumor and kill any escaped cancer cells.

In December 2010, I took a leave of absence from my veterinary career to devote myself to my new job—my survival.

Over the next several months I trusted myself to participate in my healing, whatever that meant. I gratefully received my chemo treatments envisioning them killing the cancer. I endured the initial chemo-related fevers, muscle aches, and bone pain. I celebrated my hair falling out in clumps with a short-lived pixie hair cut and beautiful scarves. I lost my body hair, my fingernails, and my memory got fuzzy. My fingers and toes went numb, my eyes constantly teared, and I lost my appetite. Eating became a tasteless chore. I kept up my daily exercise routines with the support of my boot camp buddies but allowed myself to use the "tumor excuse" when I simply lacked the strength to keep up.

My spirits remained high during my treatments and I firmly believe that staying physically active was an important part of my healing and positive attitude. Gratitude, however, played the biggest role as I gratefully accepted the loving support of generous friends and neighbors who brought meals for my family, held my hand during treatments, and delivered get-well cards, gifts, and flowers. Gratitude is a powerful healer.

During those three months of treatments, I assisted my brother with my mother's care and thoroughly explored my surgical options, interviewing five surgeons and three hospital systems. I decided to have a new type of tissue-sparing mastectomy at a world-renowned teaching hospital by a gifted surgeon. It was a great cutting-edge surgery at the time but definitely not a warm or supportive experience. With my medical knowledge, I had questions but was given minimal information and left in confusion. My emotions precipitously eroded to feelings of insignificance and distrust. I wanted my surgeon and his nurse to slow down, to see *me*, not just my cancer.

Days after my mastectomy I developed a serious post-surgical infection. The infection threatened to unravel any hope of a successful reconstruction. Fear and distrust were my painful, unhealthy companions. I was distraught by the poor communication with my surgeon and simply did not trust the conflicting information I was getting. Healing at my best was not possible in my current state of mind. I knew I could not change how my surgeon interacted with me, nor could I change the culture of the hospital so I seriously considered switching surgeons and hospitals.

Over the next several weeks of aggressive antibiotic therapy, I took responsibility for my healing. Switching surgeons midstream would come with its own complications and no guarantee for a better outcome. The only change I could control was to create change in me—how I chose to show up and *feel*. With the wisdom and guidance of Caroline Myss, and her book *Defy Gravity*, I meditated and focused on reinventing my relationship with my surgeon (and my life). I surrendered to the situation, embracing all of it, and actively flipped my state of mind from fear and anger to love and trust. This was not easy. It required constant reminding at first but the benefits were powerful and freeing. My surrendered state of love, trust, and gratitude had a momentum and staying power of its own. Simply put, I made a choice to TRUST it All and to fully accept my surgeon as a person. I consciously re-thought of him as a loving human who dedicated his life to curing and repairing desperate and often dying patients. This courageous man worked tireless hours as a surgeon, researcher, and teacher. I genuinely fell in love with him when I stepped out of my story (ego) to view him through the lens of appreciation. I softened and relaxed in my follow-up visits and gifted him with sincere appreciation, humorous cards, his favorite scotch, and my charm. He was confused at first, but then he slowed down. He got to know and care about me as a person. This amazing gift—being a person that mattered rather than one of many patients—was critical to my "survival." I subsequently healed and had successful reconstructive surgery three months later.

I have been a scrapper throughout my life, trying hard, often too hard. I usually got what I wanted, but what I got was rarely how I thought it should feel. *It was the feeling I was seeking, not the goal.* Honestly, I did not know who or what I was meant to BE or even where I belonged. I had been defining my successes by the benchmarks and opinions of others, and I never felt *good enough.* I had been tolerating my life rather than living it fully. I had been taking care of everyone and everything but myself. Facing my mortality led me to really look at my life and what was truly important *to me.* Once I stopped resisting what was happening with my cancer management (my metaphor for my life) and completely surrendered to each moment, I became flooded with feelings of gratitude, trust, and acceptance. That choice felt like freedom. Each day became a new adventure to embrace. Each day became a gift.

What surprised me most in this entire journey was how easy it was once I completely surrendered; that it was there all the time, this appreciation, sense of gratitude, love, focus, and grace. By deciding to bring healing consciousness to my experience, I was able to move through with more ease and peace than if I'd stayed stuck in the fear, denial, and overwhelm that is often the response to cancer. Facing my inevitable mortality finally woke me up to this precious gift we call life, to finally *BE in the Flow of the NOW*, and to experience it ALL (the pain as well as the joy).

*We are all going to die. When we grasp the profoundness of our mortality, we see our significance in a new light. We see the significance of everyone and everything. Death becomes an ally, a mysterious destination we will all experience when our work here in this dimension is complete.*

When most of my treatment was finished, I hired Tambre Leighn, a life coach who works with cancer survivors and caregivers. I knew I wanted to remain in the veterinary field but I did not want to simply return to general practice. Tambre's insightful questions and confidence in me were contagious, inspiring, and effective. I recognized the power of her coaching skills and knew then that I had to learn this skill set and bring it into my profession in a meaningful way. As a veterinarian, I worked with clients who were seeking their best solution to emotional and difficult situations. Often the best medical advice is not the best holistic advice, frequently provoking feelings of guilt, uncertainty, and regret. People usually know what their best answers are but fail to access them because they are stuck in the paralyzing emotional mindset of fear, guilt, shame, etc. So I pursued my certification in coaching and Energy Leadership™ in order to help people navigate the emotional challenges associated with their pets and to allow them to identify and focus more clearly on what they actually want to experience and *feel*.

On November 11, 2011, exactly one year after I discovered my cancer, I founded Veterinary Care Navigation™ and started my coach training with iPEC, Institute for Professional Excellence in Coaching. In 2013, while working with a national service dog organization, I founded EnHABiT™ (Engaging the Human Animal Bond in Tandem) to enhance the power of our bonds with our animal companions.

Fast forward. I am now blessed to say I am a breast cancer survivor and a different person. The experience of facing my mortality brought me clarity about what really matters in life. I gained a new dimension of emotional awareness and gratitude. Now, by living my life with authenticity, grace, and faith, I am able to give back and serve through the enriching emotional connections we share with each other and our pets.

## Discussion Questions

1. How do you deal with life? In what type of circumstances do you find yourself just "plowing through" in order to get things done or simply persist in struggle? Remember a time when you were really struggling. How did you feel? What was the result?

2. Think of another time or circumstance where you were fully present and allowing life to unfold. How did you feel? What else was different?

3. How do you participate in your own healing—mentally, physically, spiritually, and emotionally? What would it look or feel like to embrace your pain, illness, depression, or circumstance?

4. Think of a time when you completely surrendered to your experience with acceptance and openness to the lesson in it. Imagine what would be different for you if you stopped resisting life and decided to trust?

*Corinna Murray, DVM, CPC is a veterinarian, iPEC Certified Professional Coach, and founder of EnHABiT™ (Engaging the Human Animal Bond in Tandem) and Veterinary Care Navigation™. Corinna brings over 25 years of experience as a practicing veterinarian to these groundbreaking services dedicated to enhancing the bonds people have with their pets and the satisfaction they feel when reconciling challenges. www.drcorinnamurray.com*

Where do we enroll in Life 101? Where are the classes dealing with the loss of a job, the death of a loved one, the failure of a relationship? Unfortunately, those lessons are mostly learned through trial by fire and the school of hard knocks.

– Les Brown

ANGELA RODRIGUEZ

# Kindsight Is 20-20

The shrill ring of my cell phone blared out into the darkness, beckoning me to answer. I awoke in a fog, fumbling for my glasses and the cell phone at the same time. It was approximately 3:00 a.m. I don't know why I thought my glasses would bring some clarity to why my cell phone was ringing at this hour. Nevertheless, that dark feeling came over me, the one that says, "No good news comes at this hour." Caller ID let me know it was my sister. At that hour it was most likely a "butt dial" or, once again, she had a financial emergency and I'm the loan officer.

I gingerly answered, "Hello?"

My sister's guttural voice exclaimed, "She's goooooooooooone!" in between deep sobs, then once again, "She's gone."

Those two words made absolutely no sense to me.

All I could muster was, "Who's gone? What are you talking about?"

My sister responded, "Angelique."

My middle niece's name is Angelique. We've had a very special connection from birth. Not only was she the middle child like myself, she was a spirit to be reckoned with from early childhood on. She was the light that entered every room, the child who was the *adult* in my sister's family. She was my namesake, my sweet baby niece, my heart.

Angelique had recently met a boy who was 22. As my niece was almost 18, my sister allowed them to date. Following Angelique's life on Myspace and Facebook, I could see that she had finally found some happiness in the love arena with this young man. He appeared very caring and attentive towards her. They went a lot of places, made a lot of faces to the camera, and were kissing, laughing, and hugging in almost every photo. She had my blessing to date him. Angelique had graduated high school three weeks prior, worked at an ice cream parlor, and was preparing for college. She was popular, beautiful, outgoing, fun, and inspiring. Angelique was on top of the world.

When my sister said, "She's gone," I immediately thought, oh, she ran off with that boy. She had turned 18, the age that legally turns on the adult button in most young people's minds. In my mind, "she's gone" meant she had probably run off to elope.

I responded, "Where did she go?"

My sister angrily yelled into the phone, "NOOOOO! She's gone. She's DEAD!"

Like a vinyl record where the needle scratches and drags across it, my breath stopped. My eyes immediately filled with tears which poured over like Niagara falls, and I felt hot tears drop uncontrollably down to the soft, white comforter surrounding me.

What happened? How could this happen? When did this happen? Why was she just calling me now? Who? Why? All these questions came flooding at the same moment. I was only able to ask, "How?"

This young man, my niece's love, had offered her ecstasy (also known as MDMA, which is a neurotoxic and empathogenic amphetamine). Angelique, being young, naïve, and a pleaser, ingested it.

It was later discovered that after taking the drug, Angelique informed her boyfriend she wasn't feeling good, and went to lie down. Her boyfriend and another boy had also taken ecstasy, so they were having their own euphoria, and never went to check on Angelique.

When the boys finally realized Angelique was still *sleeping*, they did go check on her, only to find her unresponsive and lifeless. With panic striking every chord in their bodies, they dragged Angelique to her car and drove her to the hospital. Angelique was dead on arrival.

My sister had remained at the hospital, unable to pull herself away from her daughter's still body. As I listened to her sobs, every ounce of blood drained from my head as oxygen was not reaching my brain. I had to pull it together before I fainted. My youngest niece Alexandria took the phone from her mom, and all I heard was the pain and attempt of strength in her childlike voice. She said one word, "Auntie," then broke into sobs.

Disbelief rang in my ears. My heart broke in half at that moment. Reality was distant but keeping me in my body.

After ten minutes of crying, I told my sister I'd call our mom and let her know. I had to swallow again. I needed to digest the information that had just attacked my very soul.

I stood and felt like I had a hangover. I was emptied of all emotions. Hollow and numb. Circled by that fog, I went on autopilot. I called Mom, a few friends, the airline, made arrangements for doggy day care, and flew to my sister's side in Arizona.

As I slowly walked up her driveway, she opened the door, our eyes locked with knowing, and we fell into each other's arms. We cried for some time, than I had to get away from all the good-intentioned family and friends, who were attempting to create some normalcy. I had to be with my Angelique.

I asked for some private time and went to her bedroom. I expected to open the door and drop to the floor in grief. Instead, I sat on her bed. I looked around her room and breathed in all the material things that made her happy. I saw all the fun clothes and jewelry, the books, the letters and cards, the perfume and makeup, the pictures. I went through the items on her dresser. I lay on her bed and hugged her pillow. I took a deep breath of her scent which lingered on a shirt on the floor. I opened her closet and ran my hand along her clothes. I still felt her life force emanating from them. I read poetry she had created; I took a nap in her room. When I awoke, I fully awoke to the fact that her earthly body truly was no more.

As a survival mechanism, I disconnected myself from the pain in order to protect my sensitive heart. I allowed myself to become numb simply to deal with what was before me.

Perhaps because I am a police officer, I am considered the "strong one" in my family. I am the one who is expected to step up during crisis and take control; therefore, I took the helm and was the speaker at Angelique's memorial service. Because she was loved by so many, we had to utilize the school auditorium to accommodate everyone. Her friends made and wore T-shirts with her glowing face on them.

I wore black that day; however, I placed a bright faux flower on one side of my hair, like my niece used to wear. I spoke after the priest. I looked into the eyes of my family sitting in the front row and saw deep grief and relief that I was up there speaking for our family. I took a deep breath then I gave my eulogy. I attempted to keep it uplifting by mixing a reading of the usual sad funeral poem and bits and pieces of the beautiful person Angelique was. I explained how I found a little red pail in her room which had Post-it®-

size notes folded in half. On the pail were the words "bucket list." The notes ranged from "slide down a fire house pole" to "kiss someone famous" to "save someone's life." Little did Angelique know, by her death, she had probably awoken many young people to the dangers of taking drugs. She did "save someone's life."

I asked everyone to perform a short meditation in which we sent love in the form of pink energy, her favorite color, up to the heavens to surround her. Knowing my niece, I knew that she was disappointed in herself for taking the drug which ultimately took her life, which was now causing us all so much sadness. I knew that we needed to lift her soul into ascension.

I used to wonder how I was able to be so present in a time where I just wanted to ball up and not be seen. To be so present in a time where I felt so hopeless and so helpless. Like the phrase *hindsight is 20-20*, I believe *kindsight is 20-20*—looking back with loving eyes at the "lesson" before you. Looking back with perfect vision, knowing that every experience brought to you is in loving kindness for the betterment of yourself.

I was not blessed with bearing any children myself, so Angelique was the closest thing for me to having a child. Being in law enforcement, I had experienced all kinds of death. I had also been through an ugly divorce and lost a friend/partner in the line of duty. But the loss of a child . . . I wasn't sure if I could recover from that.

I now understand that God had prepared me in the years prior for an experience which would change my life. I unknowingly was led and thankfully followed in the steps of being in the present while allowing life to unfold. Through meditation at the Zen Center of Sunnyvale I studied the way of the Buddha (thus teaching me about unattachment and the importance of breath). I took Reiki classes in order to learn about and become an energy healer, which in turn made me sensitive to energy. I was led to Science of Mind and attended Conscious Living Center in Mountain View, California, where I embodied and remembered I was loved so deeply by Spirit and that "we are all spiritual beings here on earth having a human experience." (Thank you, Reverend Jane Beach.)

All of these were and still are ways in which I use my "tool belt of life." I believe we all choose our human experiences before we are born. Angelique chose to live her beautiful life, but to also allow it to expire at an early age in order to touch us all so deeply with the love of our faith. With faith, I was able to move through this experience with a knowing that I would feel whole again and have peace, which began with forgiveness on many levels. Being present and truly allowing every feeling during that challenging time has only made me and my faith stronger.

Now when adversity, challenges, and bumps in the road occur, I still myself in the presence of the All Knowing and understand these are often the first signs that a great healing has begun.

As Ram Dass, an American contemporary spiritual teacher and author of one of my favorite books *Be Here Now* says, "The best preparation for later is to be fully present right now."

## Discussion Questions

1. When have you operated from survival mode? How did that make you feel?

2. When have you had to be strong for someone else? What were your thoughts and emotions? If you could repeat that situation, what would you change?

3. What does being "present" mean? What spiritual or energetic practices help you to be more present?

4. How does the phrase "Kindsight is 20-20" apply to you? What did you learn from those lessons? How can you more lovingly look at your current lessons?

*Angela Rodriguez is Sergeant of Police for the San Francisco Police Department, a career that came about through realizing her gift of truly listening with a compassionate heart. To balance her uniformed duties, she practices Science of Mind and is also an Advanced Reiki Practitioner.*

The most beautiful people we have known are those who have known defeat, known suffering, known struggle, known loss, and have found their way out of the depths. These persons have an appreciation, a sensitivity, and an understanding of life that fills them with compassion, gentleness, and a deep loving concern. Beautiful people do not just happen.

– Elizabeth Kubler-Ross

TERRY CRUMP
# Invisible

There have been protracted periods in my life where I have been under duress, struggling significantly with my physical and emotional health. But, like many, I chose only to present a stoic or brave mask of peace. One of my major struggles has been living with a chronic illness since the outset of my adult life. By the age of 22, I was diagnosed with multiple sclerosis. For many years it was relatively benign. Over time, however, the illness viciously began to attack my spinal column, weakening the right side of my body and making movement extremely difficult. It became hard to even hold a pen or write more than a few words. I experienced unparalleled exhaustion, perpetual headaches and dizziness, awakening daily to feel as though a fleet of commercial trucks had just driven over my body, and making it difficult to even sit up from a reclined position in my bed.

Each day I felt worse and worse, despite compliance with my monthly "torture sessions," as I affectionately called my IV infusions of either steroids or Tysabri. Unfortunately, I have veins that hide and/or roll, thereby requiring more poking and prodding or multiple sticks. Thus the "torture" label. Prior to that I had been taking a medication that required once weekly intramuscular injections with very long, thick, panic-inducing needles; I was one of the fortuitous individuals who never adjusted to the meds so I could count on starting to feel feverish, exhausted (yes, even more than usual) and achy at or about eight hours following every single injection.

Despite my affinity for denial, it became glaringly evident—by my daily sobbing as I lay in a fetal position on the floor, earnest cries to God to take me from this Earth, ability to tear up at the sight of the most innocuous scene on television or elsewhere, and retreat from engaging in activities outside my home—that I was depressed. I worked from home full-time as a psychologist and managed to perform well in my assigned role, though I wasn't doing the work that I thought I'd be doing at this early stage of my career. While I grieved over my feelings of professional inadequacy, I couldn't imagine relying on this deteriorating body (that I had come to loathe) to leave the house daily, deal with horrendous daily traffic, and work in a high-paced environment like a medical hospital or residential facility, both settings that I have truly loved in the past.

With much effort, I carried on conversations with others, both family and friends, never letting on about my internal struggle. I hated when the phone rang, but I answered because I didn't want to face questions about whether I was alright or have others speculate that something was wrong. Keep it (conversations) short and superficial was my motto! This pain, isolation, depression, and self-loathing went on for many, many months, amplified by the belief that as a trained mental health professional I should be able to "heal myself."

Divine intervention came through my interactions with two close friends. One commented on the fact that I was functionally depressed, which forced me to acknowledge, out loud, what I already knew. The second came from my dearest friend, who somehow intuitively recognized my hopelessness and asked in the middle of a conversation, "You know that God doesn't have you here to suffer, right?" I hesitated to answer because I didn't KNOW that. My underlying belief was that yes, I awakened each day for the sole purpose of being tortured by ever-increasing loss of ability and the resulting mental anguish. I saw my body as decrepit. How was it that I, a Christian woman, who should be a reflection of victory over death and the grave, a woman who should be filled with joy unspeakable, could be filled with such despair that she would plead or attempt to barter daily with God to allow her to die? I reasoned that I was the epitome of a bad Christian who would never fulfill her life's purpose, so I might as well be gone. Each time I heard scriptures that referenced that God's plan was to have me prosper and not to harm me or that his grace was sufficient, I cringed. My reality was starkly different and that infuriated me.

Somehow the realization that others could see my pain prompted me to act. I made a call, scheduled a meeting with my pastor, and poured out my heart. She advised me that just because I wasn't in perfect health didn't mean that my healing would not come. In the meantime, she advised me to get busy doing the things that were of service to others. I heard her, but I couldn't imagine where I would get the energy when often I had to pray with every tenuous step that I would remain upright, using limbs that felt like dead weight. Brushing my teeth with my right hand, the weak side, was a production.

I started to research online alternative approaches to address my symptoms. Eventually my exposure to other disciplines like chiropractic care and acupuncture brought hope. Following up with appointments with various practitioners I began to experience some symptom relief. I continued living in the carefully controlled comfort and serenity of my condo, peering out the window and observing others "do life." I witnessed others' careers exploding with success, their families expanding, heard about their travels and movement and activity. I admired and longed for the same, but those sentiments were brushed off. Again, for many months I was complacent, slightly more active, but largely isolated.

The most significant turning point for me came unexpectedly on a holiday. I was enjoying the day off, watching a service in tribute to Martin Luther King Jr. that also celebrated the achievements of some very bright, active adolescents in the community who were embarking on their collegiate studies. I was inspired by the vigor and vibrancy of these youths, remembering for the first time in over a decade my own zeal at that age. Very clearly, I heard these words: "Your disability is not an excuse for invisibility." Whoa! I pondered the increasing desire I had to return to clinical work through a private practice and contemplated how I wanted to teach more at the university where I sometimes provided instruction. Although I still didn't trust my body, I really wanted to travel again, attend plays, exercise (maybe not running, but something), and do all the things that once filled me with joy. I even thought about my self-consciousness with walking in crowds or in front of others where my gait would be observed and how that was a prominent reflection of how much I would try to shrink away, wishing that I were invisible because it was too painful to think about how I appeared to others. In my own assessment, I WAS NOT the picture of a young, successful, educated, attractive, and well-deserving doctor of psychology. I wanted for my shame to be visible to no one. I did not want to be seen.

How could a loving God with plans not to harm me and give me hope allow this debilitating disease to persist, insidiously robbing me of my freedom to move, to be? I cried for my soul to be released from a body that seemed to be increasingly useless, or, at best, unreliable and extraordinarily frustrating.

Through long periods of searching and self-reflection, I have finally learned that there is beauty in vulnerability and that my faith never failed me. Even in those moments when I felt so despondent and disconnected from hope, it was my faith and continued conversations with God—yes, even the frequent angry outbursts—that brought me through.

There is no escaping the dark moments that inevitably come in life. Sometimes they are fleeting, other times they are extended periods where a sense of hopelessness pervades. I could not minimize my grief or sadness about my life course during these instances. Though painful, I had to experience the depth of it, fully. I have been forced from invisibility to visibility, from inertia to activity, called to serve even with my limitations. I have truly learned that *you don't get to hide.*

## Discussion Questions

1. How does faith facilitate, complicate, and/or impede acceptance of illness or any other life challenge?

2. In some religious traditions, the idea of "being still" is critical to adapting to a life challenge. Discuss the tension between living in "stillness" and needing to find answers to the why or for what purpose this is happening in your life.

3. Where have you been invisible in your life? What would it look or feel like to be visible?

*Terry Crump, PhD, is a licensed clinical psychologist, board certified clinical hypnotherapist, and owner of Crump Wellness Services which serves the Metro Atlanta region. She specializes in working with individuals with acute and chronic medical illnesses and provides individual psychotherapy to clients with a wide range of concerns. www.crumpwellness.com*

When we are in touch with our creativity, through passion and excitement, we always put ourselves in the most expansive state of consciousness. Fear slows down our development, while love supports a rapid growth.

— Raphael Zernoff

AZIZI BLISSETT

# The Art of Expression

From a very young age, I had a certain shyness and aloofness. I also resonated with a deep sense of fear and distrust of others, including family and friends. Well into my adulthood, I sought security in other things and people. I felt detached from my inner being and controlled by others around me. Oftentimes, I felt trapped inside my own body, completely disconnected from the outside world. I honestly did not feel like I belonged anywhere.

I grew up in a civil rights activist environment that dominated my physical, mental, and emotional state of being. However, I had always found excitement and joy in going to school because I felt a sense of freedom and imagination in the possibilities of the future. I attended a Visual and Performing Arts school from 3rd grade through high school. I studied ballet, tap dance, theater, and vocal music; played the violin and piano; and became an avid fashion design student. School was the one place I felt a sense of belonging.

In spite of that belonging and internal growth through school, my emotional and mental struggles with my family's expectations of me eventually drove me away after college and led me into a controlling and manipulative relationship.

At the tender age of 27, my boyfriend of several years proposed to me and I was very excited about our new beginning. I began planning our wedding and preparing for what I thought would be a healthy and happy marriage. On the surface, my life appeared picture-perfect. I was engaged to a smart, nice-looking young man and we both had successful careers, yet I still felt unfulfilled and hollow on the inside. Early in my career, I achieved many business accolades and was awarded with a prominent leadership role. Despite the success, I had a longing to discover my life's passion and purpose. After almost five years in the corporate world, I decided to leave the security of my job to pursue a creative career in advertising.

While I had grown significantly over the years through self-help books and caring people in my life, I thought pre-marital counseling would help my fiancé and I adjust to our new beginnings. Although I did not know what to expect, I was anxious to plan out our future together.

I quickly learned how naïve I was. I remember one specific session where the counselor asked about my childhood. I opened my mouth and no words came out. Then out of nowhere, I started to cry uncontrollably. It was quite embarrassing. The counselor was rather perplexed and began to dig deeper. The more questions she asked, the more emotions burst out of me, making it difficult to clearly communicate any words. At one point, she said to me, "you have the emotions of a four-year-old."

Those words resonated with me deeply and would eventually reconnect me with a repressed childhood trauma that remains vague to this day. I learned through counseling that I suffered from emotional suppression as a defense mechanism. It created an energetic blockage that caused my feelings to sink deep inside with no outlet for expression.

My former husband ultimately left counseling because he saw little value in it. This was the beginning of the end of a difficult and troublesome marriage. I continued to go to counseling by myself. I now had open wounds and I wanted to piece myself together one way or another.

In addition, I slowly began to cope with the failing health of my mother. She suffered from chronic high blood pressure and diabetes, which resulted in long-term dialysis treatments and other health complications. Her illness was difficult to accept and witness, as she represented strength, vitality, and a truly creative visionary to me. It was hard for me to see this renowned artist in this debilitating state. My mother's death at such a relatively young age created an overwhelming desire in me to honor her artistic legacy.

My love of the arts led me to a postgraduate school to study advertising. I was near completion of my program when I decided to take an optional class aptly titled Emotive Design. In this course the students randomly picked an emotive word from a cup and created a storybook that depicted the chosen word and its opposite. One by one each student drew a word. I remember words like Happy, Joy, and even Love. I became excited as my turn approached. I reached into the cup, unfolded the piece of paper, and silently read my word. Shame. Not Happy, not Joy, or any of the other positive emotions my fellow students picked but Shame. I was utterly confused. "What does shame have to do with me?" I can remember saying. I thought this must be a mistake. I simply did not know how I was going to produce a heartfelt, emotive design storybook with a word that had no meaning to me.

In spite of my hesitation to work on the assignment, I decided to give it my best. Each week we needed to show progress on our storybook and each week I had no progress to show. I grew frustrated and defeated. One day while I was interning at a different teacher's design studio, I explained to this teacher that I was struggling on a project in another class. As I began to describe the project, her cheerful personality jumped right in to assist me. I now had less than a week to produce something about Shame and I was willing to accept whatever assistance she offered. Within moments, she led me outside her studio to an open grassland area.

We talked more about my project as the beautiful sun beamed down on us. She then guided me through a meditation exercise where she asked me to visualize my little girl inside. Not knowing where this was leading, I decided to allow myself to let go and go inward. She asked me to use my imagination to connect with that little girl and allow whatever emotions were in her to flow through. She also asked me to imagine the words, images, and colors that came to mind as we continued the meditation. I don't know if I was able to imagine anything at all; however, I did feel a sense of freedom and peace when we were done. We hugged, went back inside the studio, and I completed my day's work before leaving to go home.

That night I had a burning desire to work on my Shame project. I gathered all of my art supplies, spiritual books, quotes, and other miscellaneous objects I had in my possession and I started painting with no beginning or end in mind. One canvas after another, I became fully immersed in the moment of creating. The emotions, images, and colors I had imagined during my earlier meditation came bursting out of me. And I was so excited! Oddly enough, I was especially excited that I had found my Shame story. I found it! So I kept creating and creating because somehow I needed to get to the other side to depict the opposite of Shame. I felt anger and created a canvas on anger. I felt fear and created a canvas on it. As I finished one canvas, the next emotion would emerge. Eventually, I began to feel the opposite of the negative emotions. I felt love and created a love canvas. I felt forgiveness and created a forgiveness canvas. My soul was overjoyed! I had found the missing piece to my life puzzle. I was whole now. And I was reconnecting with my little girl. It didn't matter to me that she was troubled and an emotional wreck when I found her. What mattered most was that I no longer felt broken and detached from my inner self. I had just tapped into my soul and divine essence. When daybreak came I was still creating. I had completed 11 pieces of art filled with raw and authentic emotions. My Shame storybook was finally finished. And almost instantly, I felt a new me emerge.

As I grew stronger over the years, my emotional wounds and heart began to heal. Finding that little girl inside of me healed a place of brokenness that the adult me didn't even know existed. It took me beyond my physical self to a new level of consciousness. By reconnecting to my soul and true nature, I was able to understand how my past choices stemmed from fear and emotional insecurity and how those choices created the controlling and emotionally abusive circumstances in my life.

I gave myself permission to release the destructive feelings and negative experiences that dominated my life and create new imaginations that were more positive and productive. I experienced the power of forgiveness. It is *the* most precious gift that I have given myself. It has freed me from my past and allowed me to reach for my dreams and to live out my purpose of inspiring others to do the same. I learned that I am not defined by my experiences, but by my desires and aspirations. And my spiritual quest has given me a peace that surpasses understanding, a reassuring peace that allows me to know that God is real and living inside of me and has been with me all the while.

Creativity through art became a form of self-empowerment for me that transformed my negative beliefs to build a self-sufficient and independent life. Using my artistry and healing story as a catalyst, I founded an organization called ZFusion, which allows me to remain connected to my true nature and creative spirit and inspire others to do the same. The "empowerment through art" workshops allow participants to use their imaginations and positive thinking to release negative thought patterns in a fun and creative way. I am also a Law of Attraction Life Coach. As a Life Coach, I show how beautiful Divine Beings like you can shift your thoughts and feelings to focus on attracting and manifesting the life that you truly desire. I not only rejoice in my own transformation; I share in the joy of the spiritual journey of others.

## Discussion Questions

1. What childhood experience or trauma has colored your view of life? What negative beliefs or feelings about yourself or life stem from that experience?

2. Visualization allows the mind and heart to work together freely. How have you used visualization to examine those negative beliefs? What revelations resulted from the visualization?

3. Art can be used as a way to release repressed emotions and transform negative beliefs. When have you allowed yourself free expression through art? If you haven't experienced this, what's standing in the way of that true expression? What fear or limiting belief comes up for you?

*Azizi Blissett is a Law of Attraction Life Coach who empowers clients to shift limiting thoughts and beliefs to live a fulfilling life. As the Founder and President of ZFusion, a 501(c)(3) organization, Azizi uses art and creativity to promote self-empowerment and emotional independence for women and youth. www.zfusion.org*

I believe that imagination is stronger than knowledge. That myth is more potent than history. That dreams are more powerful than facts. That hope always triumphs over experience. That laughter is the only cure for grief. And I believe that love is stronger than death.

– Robert Fulghum

BARBARA J. HOPKINSON
# Signs of Hope

I wasn't very spiritual twelve years ago as I walked into my twenty-one-year-old-son Brent's hospital room. I remember thinking "How could I be losing another son?" I couldn't believe what I was seeing. My Arizona State University student lay perfectly still, hooked up to life support. I'd lost his younger brother, Robbie, a full-term-stillborn son, fifteen years earlier, and had a miscarriage before that. This couldn't be happening again!

Brent had an amazing life planned. He was smart, creative, and athletic. We lived in Massachusetts but he attended military high school in New York at his request and earned a full Army ROTC scholarship to his top choice college. He was then a junior at ASU.

Brent was engaged to a wonderful woman, Laura. He had already passed his aviation written test, was ready to pass the physical test, and was prepared to serve at least eight years active duty in the military while he and Laura got married and hopefully blessed us with grandchildren. Then one May morning he borrowed a friend's motorcycle and lost control of it. Those dreams disappeared on the ASU campus in the Arizona heat, on the way to breakfast with his ROTC buddies—only three weeks after we'd taken him to Las Vegas to celebrate his 21st birthday.

After Brent's funeral, I had difficulty functioning. I didn't know what to do but knew I had to do something. I felt in my heart that helping others would help me heal. I was also driven to find out if my son's spirit continued—if he was "okay." As a parent, your number one job is to protect your children, and when you can no longer do that, it's truly devastating. Any confirmation of their spirit or well-being is a huge relief.

I spent time in therapy and deep discussions about the meaning of life with some of my more questioning spiritual friends. They educated me on their beliefs and pointed me to resources to start exploring my own faith. They stuck with me while I challenged everything that I believed and while I lived through the disbelief, sadness, and anger.

My mother's death was my first personal awakening to evidence of an afterlife. Near the end of her life, Mom was in a semi-comatose state and unresponsive. I was alone with her one day when she came out of that state, wide-eyed, to tell me she'd just seen my deceased father and her parents, who were all waiting for her. She looked so peaceful. I could tell it was very real to her. The next morning, she was up and around like nothing had happened, and then she died the following day. The look on her face convinced me that she had seen my father and grandparents and knew she would be all right. I listened to my heart, but still I had doubts.

Do our spirits continue after death? I was on a mission to find out. I'd been a skeptic from the corporate world, not thinking much about any of this before Brent's death. I forced myself to have an open mind and started reading books on afterlife, energy, and spirituality. I learned to meditate. I started journaling. I went to many varieties of energy healers. I attended spiritual development workshops, did yoga classes, walked on the beach and in nature. I spent time with psychotherapists, hypnotherapists, and mediums. The universe showed me that I had trusted friends with paranormal capabilities who could give me messages from Brent. And once I was open to it, I received signs!

I remember feeling weird going to my first medium, one that was referred. Pat was retired, but she agreed to see me at a mutual friend's request. She seemed very "normal" and knew so many details about my son and my parents (unknown to my friend) that even my more skeptical husband couldn't dismiss her. Plus she knew of something that happened at Brent's funeral, which I did not remember but my husband verified.

Six months after Brent's death, we went with some spiritual friends to do group meditations in nature. One of these trusted friends, Kathleen, was a nurse who communicated messages from Brent. After one of our meditations, she described two things she'd never actually seen before—the flowers he gave me for Mother's Day that year and a lanyard keychain from his college that I had placed in his casket before closing it and not told anyone about. She didn't even know what that object was!

After a round of mediums to validate the existence of Brent's spirit, I moved on to a round of classes to teach myself to communicate with him. I saw improvement, especially in my intuition, but my instructor told me that I needed more regular quiet time to improve further. I found that difficult. However, interactions with Brent during these sessions became almost conversational. He would interrupt the medium leading the class, who would ask me things like "were you doing anything related to Singapore today?" Odd, but yes, I'd been planning a business trip there. The medium responded, "Brent wants you to know he was with you then." Okay!

I later "coincidentally" met and became friends with a hypnotherapist and medium, Janet, who said Brent asked her to explain to me how important it was to focus on the love and the positive memories for me and all bereaved parents. She helped me understand that it's not good for any of us to hold on to the pain too tightly, that our children want us to heal. Also, their spirits are on a high vibration level of energy, at the level of love. When we remain in the low vibration level of pain and loss it is more difficult for them to connect to us. We can have the unintended effect of holding them back from their spiritual journeys with our profound grief acting as a tether. I trusted what I was hearing and did more energy work, let go of more grief, focused on the love, and felt much better.

Then came Brent's input to my work now, helping bereaved families struggling with their grief after the loss of a child. I witnessed Nancy, my musician friend, channeling two songs from Brent. We were both surprised and emotionally affected. I hadn't known of her paranormal capabilities.

After the songs, which are on my web site, Nancy could give me messages from Brent regularly, and she did. One such message was when I'd just moved into a temporary place that she'd never seen. I took a walk before unpacking and on my return, got her text: "Brent says, 'Be careful going up your front steps, Mom.'" By now, I was used to these messages, so I smiled, shrugged, texted "Thanks," and continued walking. When I got there, the entire length of the front wooden step was cracked. If I'd put my weight on the outside edge, I might have gotten hurt. Thank you, Brent!

I have several examples of credible "signs" like this, from my own experience as well as from the bereaved families I've supported for more than ten years in the local chapter of *The Compassionate Friends* which I founded. These signs provide hope to parents, grandparents, and others that their child or loved one continues and is well.

Faith was not gained instantly. It layered and strengthened over time with each new discovery, belief, or supporting event. But it was critical that I keep an open mind to the possibilities, to new ideas, and to the restoration of my faith. I learned that a good life is all about the love. May you be blessed with faith and love!

## Discussion Questions

1.  What form(s) has grief taken in your life? What were your thoughts and emotions at that time?

2.  Have you talked with a medium or someone who channeled spirits? What signs of hope did you receive? How did that help you?

3.  Are you still holding on to the pain of a loved one who has died? How is that affecting you? What would it feel like to let go of that pain?

*Barbara J. Hopkinson helps families who struggle with grief after the loss of a child to find hope and happiness again. After losing three children, Barbara founded a local support chapter helping hundreds of families. Support is enhanced through her book* A Butterfly's Journey, *retreats, a resource center, and individualized support programs. www.abutterflysjourney.com*

Never be bullied into silence. Never allow yourself to be made a victim. Accept no one's definition of your life, but define yourself.

— Harvey Fierstein

# Living the Questions

The quote that has spoken most profoundly to me about my life is one by Rainer Maria Rilke from *Letters to a Young Poet*.

> *Have patience with everything unresolved in your heart and try to love the questions themselves as if they were locked rooms or books written in a foreign language. Do not search for the answers, which could not be given to you now, because you would not be able to live with them. And the point is to live everything. Live the questions now. Perhaps then, someday far in the future, you will gradually, without even noticing it, live your way into the answer.*

The words feel like butter to me, they are smooth and silky and speak to me about the unresolved issues in my heart—what work I should be doing, who I am, what I am supposed to accomplish with my life. Like many, I did the college thing and found a job in public relations/marketing, which was the closest I could come to defining my desire. Most of the jobs I enjoyed but they didn't fulfill me. They didn't satisfy this undefined, black hole of need in me. I was basically working because that is what society dictated you are "supposed" to do.

Over the years, I got better at targeting jobs that had more of the elements that met part of the fulfillment need which included working with people, coordinating events, being creative, having some autonomy in the way I did what I did, and creating or managing programs. Working with people allowed me to become the person people sought out when they had issues, which gave me an opportunity to use my unique listening skills to help them change their perspectives or help them feel better about themselves. The other aspects fed my creativity in setting up events or creating programs. But I needed more. It appeared I was doomed to taking a job, giving it what I could, getting bored, and moving on.

Most jobs were two to three years (the longest job I ever had was 7 years and 2 months) and two things would happen. First, my inability to authentically express myself would begin my frustration, usually with authority figures in the confines of organizational structures. I was always a quick study when it came to assessing situations and people. Within most organizations, people in power positions were not there to better the whole, but to elevate themselves or simply look good. My new boss's attitude "keep them happy and keep them out of my office" was a perfect example. I was angry, frustrated, and felt dismissed and unimportant by his relegating my contribution to the status of babysitter, but I felt powerless to say anything for fear of getting fired. Aside from the frustration, boredom would set in. Organizational structures tend to be steeped in routine and while there is comfort in that, too much routine stifles my creativity.

For 20 years, when people asked me what I wanted to do, the only description I could give them was "I want to help people." I started to dread the question. After about age 40, I tried to avoid the question altogether. But I was starting to learn, through experience, that I wanted to "help people live better." Life doesn't always give us what we want when we want it, no matter how much we agonize. For most of my adult life I've searched for how to use my talents—the gift of listening and hearing the more subtle meaning of what people are trying to convey, lifting people's spirits up to help them feel better about themselves, healing emotional wounds just by reframing past events or simply being a witness to the story, and teaching people how to think differently about life circumstances and helping to lay solid foundations wherever I am and whatever I am doing. But after years of headhunters, career coaches, and batteries of tests, I was stuck in the same thing time and time again— marketing. It wasn't until my last marketing job at the ripe old age of 55 that I got the pleasure of being "released" (a term used by corporations in Georgia when your personality is something that the boss can no longer tolerate or there isn't a good reason to get rid of you). About six months into the job, I already knew I needed to get out. Management had, in my opinion, started having unreasonable expectations in terms of sales numbers. I quickly realized my boss was going to be a force to reckon with this time. It was time to face the demons of childhood patterning and set myself free.

I've always been interested in personal improvement. When I recognized the pattern in management that was similar to my childhood issue of not being allowed to feel or express my thoughts or feelings, I knew all too well what was happening. Emotionally I felt stifled and frustrated, like when I was younger. It was even causing problems for me physically, with my feet. Energetically, I was told I was not standing up for myself. I had become all too good at stifling my feelings and opinions in lieu of challenging authority. So little by little, but professionally, I started asking questions when I thought something wasn't right. I challenged decisions made for me when people assumed they knew about my territory. Each step of the way I took more control back and began voicing my opinions and feelings. Through this expression my foot problem virtually disappeared.

It didn't take long for this to rub my boss the wrong way. Within three months, I knew I was on shaky ground and by six months I was out the door.

It never feels good when someone makes a decision about you that is less than flattering. The sheer act of being fired was enough of a social stigma without them trumping up charges.

I was the do-gooder, the generator, the person everyone comes to. The one who gets things done.

This couldn't be!

I walked out that evening after my termination to a large full moon hanging in the sky and I knew instantly that this was an ending. An ending to doing jobs that weren't fulfilling me.

The ending of that job was followed with a beginning. The beginning for me was my decision not to be profoundly miserable anymore and live the questions that will lead me to find the fulfillment I seek. Perhaps now you can see why Rainer Maria Rilke's quote spoke to me. I continue to learn patience and I am following his advice. For me, living the questions is to continue to ask myself what I like or dislike about what I'm engaged in. It is evaluating how I feel about what I'm doing and looking for ways to do more or less of it. I know that I have the strength to stand my ground and not give into my own fears or society's expectations, though it gets scary. To be strong while I'm still honing where and how my gifts will best be used in the world. To focus on

105

income-generating opportunities that allow me to use my gift for listening and to hear what people need, to help them shift perspectives and feel good about being who they are, just as they are, and helping them to build solid foundations on which to live and have faith in themselves..

Many of us attempt to move through life accomplishing more at a frenetic pace, to be measured against some standard that others seem able to achieve or exceed. If you don't achieve that standard you are made to feel that something is wrong with you. It takes great faith and courage, which can be years in manifesting, to break away from society's view of success and follow your heart to the expression in life that you are uniquely designed to be and to define your own success.

Getting out of my head feels like an unconscionable task, but I recognize and honor the longings of my heart, my soul's desire to continue to seek the authentic in me, the bare essence of who I am. My hope is that my contribution will encourage those who struggle with self-expression, self-esteem, or love of self, or who have been made to feel that expressing their true selves would be wrong. Know that it is safe to get into the waters of life and reveal the real you, no matter how long it takes.

## Discussion Questions

1.  How have you been frustrated with an inability to express yourself? What were you afraid of? What prevented you from standing up for yourself?

2.  When have you been unsure of the direction of your life? In what way did you feel stuck? What would have helped you feel more certain?

3.  How are you "living the questions"? Where do you or do you not have patience with the circumstances in your life? How can you best follow your heart to its fullest expression?

*Maureen Roe is passionate about helping others feel worthy and accepting of themselves. As author, speaker, and self-esteem coach, and creator of Done with Judging & Criticizing coaching programs, she now uses these techniques coupled with her warmth and humor to help others heal as she personally healed herself. www.maureenroecoaching.com*

Have faith in your dreams and someday your rainbow will come smiling through.

– Walt Disney, Cinderella

LORELEI ROBBINS
# Dreams Do Come True

"Walk on, walk on with hope in your heart, and you'll never walk alone . . ." That song from *Carousel* accompanied me on my journey as a young child growing up in an upper middle class neighborhood in Manhasset, Long Island. I wandered alone during the summers waiting for school to start because I had no friends. I was convinced that my parents were the only divorced couple and that we were the only "broken family" in the neighborhood. Whether this was true or not, who knows, but it sure did fit my journey of feeling abandoned, not belonging, and not fitting in. And even though I felt lonely and disenfranchised, deep down I believed that if I wished hard enough, my dreams would come true. Little did I know that was the beginning of the role that I now play as a Dream Accelerator for others.

As a child, I never wanted to leave my room. I felt safe, nestled, and cocooned there, while the thought of venturing out filled me with terror. Yet, at the same time, one of my fondest memories as a young child was being on the radio with my dad and creating his show, Robbins Nest, from the den in our home. I was actually the youngest disk jockey in the country at four years of age.

As far back as I can remember, all I wanted was to feel that I belonged. Instead, I felt that I never fit in. I kept looking to others to please define me and tell me who I am. I looked especially to my romantic relationships and jobs to find myself.

What further added to my experience of being a misfit was when my grandparents moved me, my mother, and my sister Cathy to Switzerland so that we could benefit from a European education. And where did I wind up? In two different Catholic boarding schools in the 60s. The first was in Rorschach, the German part of Switzerland where the inkblot test originated. (Because I was shy and didn't really interact with the other kids in kindergarten, the school sent me to a psychologist who actually gave me that inkblot test when I was six. I remember thinking the guy was nuts.) We were the only Americans in a school where no one spoke English (except the Mother Superior), and we had a horrific time with showering only once a week, washing our hair only every two weeks, and going to mass three times a week. I felt grungy and on religion overload. The second school was in Fribourg, the French part of Switzerland. There were girls from all over the world here, which added to the language problem. In those two boarding schools, I learned to speak German and French.

In the search to find myself, I married five times from 1970 until 2009. As I write this, it's even hard for me to believe that, because each time I married I was certain that it would last forever, and I would at last feel safe and secure in the framework of a marriage. I would finally find myself.

I also tried desperately to find myself in all kinds of jobs. I was a college German instructor and executive assistant to some really cool folks: Vice President of Publicity and Public Relations at Bantam Books, Director of Advertising at Rolling Stone Magazine, trilingual assistant to Director of Research at Bristol Labs International. I was a travel agent, a real estate agent, an insurance agent.

It's always baffled me that despite my great need to belong, to be validated, and to be approved of, I kept being guided in a direction that was unconventional, "outside the box," and challenging to my closest relationships. Even though I've been self-employed since 1981, when I started my personnel consulting business and then my astrological business, Thank Your Lucky Stars, in 1987, I spent most of my life still trying to jump on someone else's train (bandwagon) to get their approval and validation of my worth and my value.

I did keep putting one foot in front of the other in my desire to sing my song and not die with my music in me. The irony was that the more steps I took to express myself authentically, to be me with apology to no one, the more it threatened the status quo and the safety and security of my important relationships.

I surprised myself when my fifth marriage ended just a short 15 months after it began. What did that say about me? What was I telling myself? That I couldn't get it right? Well, other than five men saying yes, which is a feat in and of itself, I knew that there must be gifts from those relationships I had yet to unwrap. So after enough guilt and shame, and comparing myself to others who had managed to have happy long-term marriages, I came to know that my marriages, just like my jobs, were my greatest teachers. In each marriage and in each job I either became more or less of myself. I either found myself or lost myself . . . mostly lost myself in those days.

After researching and studying relationships, what finally hit me like a ton of bricks was that in order to have what I most desired in my relationships, I had to become my own best partner. In other words, I had to learn that love is "being" the right partner, not "finding" the right partner. But I gotta tell you it really pissed me off. I so wanted to find the love, solace, comfort, and acknowledgement *out there* because I still didn't see it in myself. After my last marriage ended, there was a prayer from Rumi that I repeated over and over again knowing the truth of it from the depths of my being: "It's not your task to seek for love, but merely to seek and find everything within yourself that you have built against it."

I think back to my childhood and how much "little Lore" would have benefitted if she had known that her painful shyness, difficulty fitting in, and her need to be in her "sanctuary" were co-created by God and her soul before she was born. (For you astrology buffs, that means natal Libra Sun, Venus, Neptune, natal Scorpio Mercury all in 4th house).

Had I been aware of my soul's map, I would have known that once I felt comfortable and safe, the childlike/playful/showman side of me would emerge and I could easily establish rapport with other people. (Natal Mars in Leo)

But here's the awesome news . . . the fat lady hasn't sung yet. I am 67 years young. I feel better than ever emotionally, physically, and spiritually because I am doing work that really jazzes and juices me and makes a valuable contribution to people's lives. I have finally "married" (and I do not use that word lightly) my skills as a spiritual astrologer, counselor, interviewer, and minister to help people accelerate their dreams, by daring and allowing them to come true. What's so exciting now is that I have taken the best of my family legacy, from being on the air with my dad in Robbins Nest at four, and at 65 I created Robbins Cosmic Nest, where dreams that you dare to dream really do come true.

The icing on the cake is that at the Libra New Moon in October, 2012, I created the New Moon Wish that changed my life forever: *The man I desire and deserve finds me irresistible and makes my heart do a happy dance.* Did I

DARE wish for another partnership after being married five times? Maybe I had reached my relationship quota. But the dreamer in me prevailed, and in that lunar cycle I invited John, a friend of mine for 12 years, to a Scorpio birthday party. I hadn't actually dated, other than a couple of coffee dates, since my last marriage four years prior because I knew that my focus needed to be on graduate school and my inner journey of "dating myself." We had a drink before the infamous birthday party, and I said the most mature thing I had ever said to any man: "John, I just want you to know that I am open to having a romantic relationship with you." The rest, as they say, is history.

If I had known early in life that my Moon and North Node were in Taurus, I would have been more prepared to learn that when I live by my own values, I would feel good about myself, and to know that I would win when I proceed slowly and persistently, step by step, to build something of value.

The road to living an authentic life takes courage, commitment, and the willingness to be true to your own, unique path. It can be hard, really hard to stay the course and not give up, to consciously choose moment by moment to believe in who you are and what you came here to share with the planet.

The thought that I would "die with my music still inside me" has terrified me and kept me up at night. Once I became aware that the fear was actually motivating me more than the joy of "singing my song," I freed myself from my self-made prison and was able to experience the magic of my own spirit.

Daring to dream has been taking the risk over and over to sing my song no matter what. As Rumi said, "I want to sing like the birds sing, not worrying about who hears or what they think." You have come to the planet with unique gifts and talents, and when you express them, your heart jumps for joy and your soul rejoices.

## Discussion Questions

1. Do you remember a time when you felt left out and you wanted to belong? What were your thoughts and emotions?

2. Why is it important to feel valuable? What ways can you approve of and validate yourself?

3. Are you expressing yourself authentically right now? If not, what dream are you keeping inside that you want to share with others?

*Lorelei Robbins inspires people to realize their dreams by having the courage to DARE to dream, to release what's in the way, and to surrender to Divine timing. Her unique combination of talents as a spiritual astrologer, counselor, professional interviewer, and minister are all in service to helping people accelerate their dreams. www.robbinscosmicnest.com*

If you are always trying to be normal, you will never know how amazing you can be.

— Maya Angelou

LYNN REKVIG
# Back to Normal

The moment I sensed something was wrong remains etched into my memory like an imprint of an unforgettable photo. A full color, vivid, still life screenshot in my mind.

Having just arrived at my sister's home, I was standing in her kitchen and noticed a large, clear plastic bottle filled with something white and opaque. I didn't know exactly what it was, and it seemed unusual to see such a large bottle of something so unfamiliar.

My sister, Karin, was lying on the sofa in the next room. Curious about the large white bottle on the counter, I asked her what it was for. She replied, "I need to have some tests done next week."

"Some tests?"

"Yes," she answered from the other room.

I felt a bit worried as I had no idea there might be any health problems or concerns. Bewildered, I asked, "What kind of tests?"

Karin and I were ten years apart so we were not close growing up because of our age difference. However, as I grew up, the issue of age seemed to dissolve over time and we became close as friends as well as sisters.

She started nursing school when I was just 10 years old. As a registered nurse, she had been a role model to me as I was growing up. I didn't really think a lot about becoming a nurse in my childhood, but watching her grow into her profession inspired me to choose nursing as a career.

We ended up working together for several years at the same metropolitan hospital specializing in children. While we were in different departments, a number of our assigned activities overlapped and it was always a joy to share lunch or coffee together when our schedules permitted. A few years earlier, I had accepted a promotion at a larger general metropolitan hospital not too far from her home. Even though we no longer worked in the same place, we remained close and talked at least once a week or more regarding care for our mother, who was now in assisted living.

On this particular visit, I had gone to Karin's house for our usual monthly meeting to work on our mother's finances and various personal matters related to her overall health and well-being.

However, now I was concerned about my sister's health and well-being. As I walked into the next room, she began to tell me that her stomach had been bothering her for several weeks but she didn't know exactly why. She had spoken with her physician about her concerns at her previous exam but there were no clear answers. When the problems persisted, she had called her doctor again, and after another visit, she had been scheduled for further tests and an exam.

The results of my sister's exam did not bring good news. The physician reported that her scan showed a large tumor in her abdomen. They recommended exploratory surgery as soon as possible to remove the tumor and hopefully determine the cause of the problem. It was scheduled for the following week on Tuesday at 10 a.m.

The surgery took longer than expected and was quite complicated. The tumor was very large and difficult for the surgeons to remove. By the time the surgery was completed they were still uncertain of the cause of the tumor or primary source. There was a long waiting period for the biopsy and test results.

It was very difficult to wait so long for the news from the surgery. My thoughts and imagination wandered all over the place, from hoping it might just be a benign growth to thinking that it could be something with a life-threatening prognosis. Trying to concentrate at work was difficult. At times I felt like I didn't really want to be at work, yet in many ways, work provided some stability in this new sphere of uncertainty.

Waiting for the prognosis was more difficult than receiving the news. When we don't know the outcome of something uncertain, we tend to expect the worst. Perhaps it is some type of self-protective mechanism to prepare us for the worst in case that is what unfolds. In essence, it seems like not knowing a prognosis is harder than knowing the results even if the results are not good news.

About ten days after the surgery the definitive diagnosis was determined as ovarian cancer. While I didn't know much about the details of the prognosis, my inner dialogue and thoughts were positive, believing that she was going to be okay. I kept thinking about her overall healthy state of being. She was trim and physically active and in the prime of her life, with four grown children. In my opinion, she was living a balanced life. She had a lot of creative hobbies like knitting, weaving, and sewing. She was great at cooking and baking and she was an avid golfer.

Once Karin healed from the surgery, chemotherapy was started. The two years that followed were a roller coaster ride of ups and downs as my sister travelled on her journey with her illness. At the time of her diagnosis, there were not many treatment options available for ovarian cancer. The chemotherapy that Karin received had a lot of negative side effects. In addition to the chemotherapy, she also needed additional surgeries and other treatments. To say it was painstaking to watch her suffer is an understatement. At some of the most difficult times during her illness, I felt so much anguish. There were moments I sincerely wished that I could step into her shoes and just trade places to relieve her of some of her pain and suffering. But she never complained.

One of my clearest memories was that Karin remained so strong and resilient. One of the answers that I found in my heart is that her stalwart faith in God gave her the strength to continue with unwavering confidence. While we shared our Christian faith together, I was astounded at her courage to continue to take each day without complaining or falling apart. I am not sure that I could have done the same. Once again, she became a role model for me.

Two years after being diagnosed, Karin passed away peacefully in her home on hospice care. That day she was surrounded by her loving family members. While I was not able to be with her at the moment of her passing, I was at her bedside the night before she died and then again early the next morning. Even though saying goodbye to her that morning was heart wrenching, it helped that she knew I was there with her. And, because of our shared faith, I knew in my heart and soul that someday we would be joined together again.

There were aspects of my journey with Karin that created shifts in my perspectives on life. The first thought has certainly been said before: control is an illusion. This was one of the most difficult things to realize. I sincerely believed there must be something I could do to help Karin in her desire to live. But in the end there was absolutely nothing to do except to be with her.

Even though I had no control, I did begin to see the hidden gifts in day-to-day living. Life can become very short, very fast, and without much notice. Living, in the present moment, took on a whole new meaning to me. Just being able to be with Karin, even if I didn't know what to do or say at certain times, was something I cherished. Those moments in my memory of our time together have become like sacred gifts.

When you lose someone you love, consider that life may not go "back to normal" as you might imagine. When you lose someone that had an important place in your life, how can life ever really go "back to normal"? Over time, however, you may awaken to some new realizations in your own life as a result of the loss. And hopefully, along your journey you'll be able to discover that despite the loss, you have come through by finding answers in your own heart.

## Discussion Questions

1. When have you wanted to trade places with someone in order to ease that person's pain or anxiety? How did you find the strength to carry you through that ordeal?

2. When have you felt out of control in your life? Is feeling "in control" an illusion? How does being "in control" help or hinder your life?

3. Describe what "normal" means to you. How does the state of "normal" change with time? How does your attachment to "normal" help or hinder your life process?

*Lynn Rekvig, founder of Optimal Outcomes R$_x$, shows people how to get unstuck by helping them remove the barriers holding them back from achieving their goals and life dreams. Lynn's genuine heart-centered compassion creates a safe space for her coaching clients to experience profound growth and personal transformation.*

Perhaps the most liberating moment in my life was when I realized that my self-loathing was not a product of my inadequacy but, rather, a product of my thoughts.

— Vironika Tugaleva

JUDY KEATING
# The Way Home

I was born with a neurological disorder—cerebral palsy. When I was young I went through years of physical therapy, braces, night braces, and clunky shoes. In my late twenties and early thirties I started having falling episodes that eventually resulted in broken bones. I currently use a walker, and have recently been able to move with lofstrand crutches, which may not seem like much improvement, but it is! Despite this disorder, I have lived a full life through the support of family, friends, incredible medical help, and a large capacity for love, laughter, and patience. There are challenges with my mobility and balance, but I live what most people would consider a "normal" life. I hold an advanced degree, I have worked for over thirty years in professions aligned with my education, and I am happily married.

While the first half of my life may have seemed almost impossible to the average person, it is the second half that has truly tested me. On the quest of my inner self I have put in the 10,000+ hours it takes to become an expert, honing what I consider to be my calling—listening and following my own inner loving and compassionate voice. Getting to this place has been arduous, painful, gut-wrenching work. I have battled crippling self-doubt, cruel self-loathing, and judgment worthy of a TV show (aka *Judge Judy*). The voice in my head that told me I was unworthy of love and respect almost won out, until I embraced a spiritual journey that revealed that my gift was simply in being present with people. My presence brought people incredible peace and relaxation. My husband has dubbed this "timelessness" as people take a deep breath and visibly soften when I am physically near. I also found that my most natural way of serving humanity is through energetic modalities and the use of my voice as an author and public speaker.

But I could not offer that to myself, no matter how hard I tried or pushed or efforted. The ego part of self that allows for no quiet, no place of rest, continued to overanalyze and judge myself. I believed that abusing myself was the only way to accomplish the goal of finding inner peace. And it felt awful. I just did not discern there was another way. Truly, I was living the insanity of "doing the same thing over and over and expecting a different result" more earnestly than you can imagine. I did not feel I was worth the same compassion that I could give to others as easily as breathing. And I did it without being conscious that I was doing it.

I worked 12- to 14-hour days to the detriment of my spirit, my body, my mind, and good sense. I did things I loved on the side, in my "spare time." But I was unable to find the edge between balance and growth. I mistook my requirement of efforting in the physical realm as a life sentence that "everything had to be hard" for it to be worthwhile. I easily dismissed those things that were easy and a natural part of my divine given skills and abilities. I was certainly not the fastest learner. Everyone has innate gifts, I truly believe that, and it is amazing how much time, effort, and energy it took me to accept those that I had and only I could share.

Recently, I stepped away from work that was not feeding me. I had no guarantee that I'd make rent or give my spouse the financial support that would allow us to live without worrying about money. But the cost of not doing this became too great. I needed rest and I needed to allow myself space to not worry about what I was not doing. By allowing myself time to sit in nature and move my body or exercise every day, I found a way to get more done and feel good. This gave me a better gauge on how to utilize my time working with people, projects, and creative endeavors where I felt I was offering my best work.

Despite being in my own way, I sought out experiences, teachers, and communities that taught me to get curious about my "own mischief," as the late Bill Riedler would say. Slowing down enough to really listen to what I was thinking and to ask "is that true"? For me that was being in touch with what my body needed—rest, movement, play, breathing, being in nature and being discerning enough to make the choices that made me feel good, and saying no to obligations or overworking or being with people who made me feel bad. There would be long spans of time where I would fail to pay attention. Then I would notice occasionally that those positive thoughts and actions were possible and they began to happen more often. And I found teachers, healers, and experiences where people met me where I was and liked me despite my own judgments of myself.

I finally discovered that I am here to source Source. That means I am able to access what I call the Universal inner-net. I found my GPS—that quiet, loving voice that nudges me that this will feel good and it's now time to pay attention. My operating system. The most profound discovery was to come to a peace around how I had functioned in the past. To practice gratitude. To be thankful for all the ways that the scared, punishing aspect of my psyche was trying to protect me rather than make it wrong or bad. To give myself permission to want what I want and to guide me in that direction. When I follow my own guidance, Spirit responds by opening up the next right step or confirming I am on the right path. For instance, several months ago I was asking Spirit about what I should do next and I got the invitation to be part of this book.

Many teachers gave me the same message: "Be in nature, let it reflect what is happening, align with nature and the elements, and your creations will birth in a natural way. Adapt to the energy system that sustains you rather than drains you. Trust yourself, and allow yourself to be a conduit of Spirit." The most profound gifts were around doing less, resting, and allowing my own inclinations and energy level to be the driver, rather than the destructive judging voice that was constantly badgering me to "do more!" In that spirit, I have found great solace in working with Crystalline Consciousness Technique™, an energy system that has enabled a significant leap forward for me. It could be considered the fuel that best resonates with making things easy for me and letting the energy work for me rather than my having to push at it to "make" something happen.

Since these revelations, I have had more opportunities to be in alignment with roles that enlivened my life force—those of coach, healer, author, facilitator, and public speaker. Because, after all, I was all of those all along. I just re-gathered all those parts of myself and can now be, do, and express them in a way that no longer taxes me. I have gotten the message that it is time to bask in all I have gathered and find an integration of all that I have become, rather than have segmented parts of myself that I share only with those that I am sure will accept what I allow them to see. I am me, fallible and grace-filled, whole and ready to embrace whatever comes next. And I am certain I am not alone. There are so many people seeking the why of their toil, time, and hours spent in unfulfilling endeavors. As someone who has walked that path, I offer peace, signposts along your way, and a map to finding your own inner knowing or, as I like to call it, your way home.

## Discussion Questions

1. Self-doubt often appears as a negative voice inside your head. When do you hear that voice and what does it say? If self-doubt were silenced, what would happen?

2. What are your divinely-given skills and abilities? When have you ignored those skills and abilities? When have you used them to further your life and dreams?

3. When are you in alignment with nature or Spirit? How does that help you find your way home?

*Judy Keating was born to contribute to others through her presence and holding a sacred container during times of grief, transformation, and transition. Her clients say that her voice, her insight, and her professional offerings result in renewed peace, ease, and the ability to move forward in their lives. www.innerlifecoaching.net*

Forgiveness releases us from the painful past.

– Gerald G. Jampolsky, MD

RICIA L. MAXIE
# From Fear to Strength

I was spending a delightful evening with friends amid coffee and conversation at a local hangout. I hadn't laughed that much in a while. Then I unceremoniously drove home and walked from the small parking lot to my door at the end of the building. Still feeling happy about my night "out on the town," I reached for the door knob and a jet stream of evil surged into my hand, gushing black and thick. An intruder. Temporarily frozen, I took an audibly forceful breath. As I turned to run, he heard that breath, ran after me, and yanked me into my apartment.

For the next two hours I was choked and punched, fought against attempted sexual assault, and was thrown against the walls like a rag doll. Weighing only 98 pounds, I fought back with fierceness, kicking my legs at any part of his body, but I couldn't escape this Caucasian man's considerable 6'3" frame. The only sounds I heard were my bones crunching against the paper thin walls and the reverberation of my screams piercing my head. My cries for help had to have been heard by every person in the building while I was tortured for two hours. Finally he had enough and dragged me by the scarf around my neck to my car while my screams shattered the otherwise quiet and sleepy night. Eyes peered out from the sterile windows next door, then the drapes were hastily pulled shut and no one came to my rescue.

He drove like a madman tightly gripping the scarf, choking me tighter from time to time. My right collar-bone was shattered, rendering my right arm useless and I remained a prisoner in my own vehicle. Threats to kill me then became his banter. "I'm going to kill you, but when I do, I'll be put to death so I'll kill both of us." The car swerved around tight curves above the jagged rocks of the inlet in what otherwise would be one of the most beautiful locations in Marin County, California.

I declared, "Oh, no you're not!" At that moment I felt a surge of power shoot through me and I grabbed the steering wheel with my left hand and swerved the car away from the cliff. Immediately afterward I blacked out.

When I came to, we were on a small frontage country road, no homes in sight. The car was beginning to decel-erate. Headlights behind us shone in the distance and the closer they got the more my captor slowed down. When the lights were right behind us he loosened his grip on my scarf. The car was still traveling at least 20 miles per hour when

I jumped out and grabbed hold of the police officer who by now was standing beside his vehicle with a rifle aimed at my abductor.

It turns out that a man three blocks in the opposite direction of my apartment parking lot called the police. This angel saved my life and it was a miracle that the police found me with an inaccurate description of my car.

With relief and gratitude, I was taken to the local police station where my body shook for more than an hour while I involuntarily sobbed. Yet I soon experienced the most incredible lack of compassion from one of the officers who commanded that I stop crying and claimed I was acting like a baby. This small, insensitive statement proved to be a precursor of the future.

It was logical for me to pursue legal justice, but family, friends, and even medical personnel believed it unnecessary. Stunned at the lack of reasonable support, I went forward anyway. I was convinced that the public defender believed that justice should take due course, but I found those to be false hopes. In addition to showing an obvious lack of compassion, he told me that I was too emotional to go on the stand. I insisted that being somewhat emotional was to be expected; I was almost killed!

Shortly into the meeting, the officer was called into the public defender's office. I'll never forget his legs spread in a strong, military-style stance, arms straight with his hands behind his back, eyes looking up and forward, never making contact with mine. When asked what he witnessed that night, he replied, "I saw nothing." I was furious and started reminding him of what happened, how he intercepted the man who almost took my life. His eyes never wavered, his stance remained the same, and his statement didn't change.

In the courtroom I stood by myself watching this criminal joke with the officers; he didn't look worried in the slightest. The judge asked a few cursory questions then glared at me as if I were the villain. "You're young, pretty, wear a short dress, and you had a child out of wedlock. You were asking for it," oozed from the judge's mouth.

Appalled, I couldn't speak. This tyrant received a sentence of only thirty days in jail. And it was suspended. He didn't have to serve any time at all. At that moment I lost faith in public safety and the justice system and I felt a swell of anger at them, at him, and at myself. How could I have been so stupid to somehow allow this—all of this—to happen?

A year later, this same serial tormenter arrived at my house with two carloads of friends. It was clear that several had been trained in combat because they surrounded my home, crawling toward the windowed doors and multiple windows. This act solidified the fear I already lived with on a daily basis. I was scared out of my mind and called 911. An eternity later an officer finally responded. The thugs scattered but the officer never came to the front door to check on me. Just a "boys will be boys" prank, he reported.

About eight years later I saw the brute at a rural bus stop. The morning sky was still dark as I waited for the bus to take me on the hour drive into San Francisco. Through the dense fog and chilled air, he came sauntering toward the bus stop. No one else was there—just him and me. I turned my head so he wouldn't recognize me and when the bus finally arrived (it felt like hours rather than minutes passed) I was relieved he didn't get on.

Normally, I would say good morning and the bus operator would respond with a quick hello. This morning was different. He took one look at me and said, "Are you alright? You look like you've seen a ghost."

"Thank you. I'm fine," I shakily replied. That morning traffic was more snarled than usual which caused the bus ride to be much longer than normal. I was ready to get on with the day and be in the comfort of my own office.

When I thanked the bus operator and stepped toward the exit, he stopped me and asked, "Are you sure you're doing okay? You still don't look alright." Even though the traffic was heavier than usual and took more time, that entire ride didn't mask my ghost-white face or the fear that filled my eyes.

Shortly after the incident at the bus stop I attended lengthy intuitive development classes that proved to be spiritually awakening and thrust me into personal growth beyond my expectation. One thing I learned was that we must take responsibility for *all* of our actions—not just some. This was a new and different concept for me at the time. I remember a man in San Francisco whom I had not previously met asking me quite out of the blue about my life. I told him I had some good times but some very difficult times, as well, and he asked how much was due to my responsibility. I immediately answered "95 percent." He just laughed. I didn't understand the laughter but soon I started making an inner inventory and taking more responsibility for the decisions in my life and asking the Divine for freedom from poor choices and this fear. I learned that these circumstances were not my *fault* but *were* the result of poor thinking thus making poor decisions and not taking responsibility to make both inner and outer changes.

After attending these personal development classes I was able to advance and attend group sessions with a different instructor who, for the next five years, helped me to see in myself what I didn't recognize on my own. Forgiveness was a major factor in releasing the anger and fear, and soon thereafter I would be put to the test.

About six years after the bus incident (fifteen years after the initial event) I was no longer working in San Francisco. I walked from my office to my husband's, two blocks away, and I saw "him" kitty-corner across the street. Time halted and I simply stared at him in disbelief. During those years of self-discovery I had worked on forgiveness of myself and others in my life, of the small transgressions and the most difficult ones, but I had no idea if I was at the state of mind to forgive him or what that would feel like. I realized I felt nothing—no fear, no hate, no anger—and it was then that I knew I had let it all go. I was elated! I ran the rest of the way, met my husband, and shared my thrilling news. I was no longer a prisoner and was finally really freed from that horrific experience many years earlier.

All this seems like another lifetime ago, as if I'm remembering it from a past life recall. But it was from this life. I've worked diligently to get to where I am and I know there will always be more to learn. The naïve, young lady has grown into a wiser, more mature woman who has grown to trust herself, as well as the Divine. My voice isn't silenced by surprise or fear; it's loud and strong with an inner power that's easily accessible. I know that through this strength I serve my daughters and granddaughters, my sons and grandsons, as a healthy role model.

## Discussion Questions

1. Describe a time in your life when you were victimized. How did that make you feel then? How does it make you feel now?
2. Did you pursue justice? If not, why not? If so, how did you feel afterwards?

3. Have you released any anger or fear around the situation? Have you forgiven the person who did you harm? If not, what is preventing your forgiveness?

*Ricia L. Maxie, M.A., is an internationally renowned intuitive consultant/mystic, Reiki practitioner, and speaker and has been providing intuitive consultations, leading spiritual retreats, and teaching classes and meditation for thirty years. www.RiciaLMaxie.com*

The human voice is the most beautiful instrument of all, but it is the most difficult to play.

– Richard Strauss

LINDA GODMAN
# Growing My Voice

LINDA GODMAN
# Growing My Voice

I have a studio photograph of a 5-year-old smiling girl that once made my core ache. What others don't see was what had led up to that photo shoot. An older cousin had taught me a smart-mouthed joke: When someone asks, "What's your name?" reply "Santa Claus, ask me again and I'll slap your jaws." I was naive, to say the least, because I thought it would elicit a laugh on that day. Instead, my dad *jerked* me out into the parking lot, away from anyone's view, and beat me with his belt. I couldn't catch my breath, I was sobbing so uncontrollably. All he said was, "Shut up. Don't you cry. Go back in and smile."

That was my handling of emotions in a nutshell for years to come. I entered elementary school without confidence, but soon found my freedom in reading and spelling bees and competing. Outwardly, everything in my four-person family was fine, but there was a reason why Mighty Mouse was my favorite cartoon character, ready to save the day. I found myself sitting out recess in the second grade after kicking a boy ahead of me in line, which was my first (and to my memory, my last) punishment at school. I was humiliated as I heard the teachers discussing me: "That's unlike her. Then she didn't tell the truth about it. What's going on?" Seven may be too young to fully incorporate "why" on a soul level, but I knew I didn't want to feel that way again. If being good was the way I would feel good, then that's what I would be. I *did* know that I wanted to experience joy and laughter, and be helpful, honest, and from then on, to treat everyone respectfully. But the how do I get from here to where I would go was yet to be determined.

For years to come, my heart seemed fullest at the piano. My grandmother kept me after school and began teaching me from old hymnals. One of my best friends was my duet partner, and we were the stars of our teacher's recitals. Coupled with that joy was the emotional turmoil I felt at moving from that rural, close-knit location. At 11, I started a new life in Perry, Georgia, a larger town further away, with my mother being the only income parent. What lay ahead for my mother was a good job, and the opportunity was there for my dad to come along if he could behave better towards us. I remember white knuckling a pillow to my chest inside the closet of a hospital following Mother's angina attack. I had seen his threat to her prior to the ambulance and I was determined to stay away from his anger and rage, which meant I probably would be distanced from his family whom I loved dearly. No one would understand, except my mother. We were the only witnesses, and I shared in her feeling of isolation. I welcomed the divorce and felt that we children could be her happiness, smiling her through each day. But financial survival came at a price. Mother baked cakes on the weekend, kept another set of books in the evenings, and at one point, tried to juggle a hostess job at a restaurant until she became too tired at her "real job." Our time together was fleeting, usually Sunday at church, and I was in charge of my brother's homework. Our school was further ahead than I'd previously experienced, and I was unkind to my brother. I had little patience with someone four years younger. I also couldn't imagine the loss he might have felt at missing his father, his male role model.

The homemade dresses from my grandmother with the sashes were no longer acceptable where I lived, so a fabric store became my regular outing, and I developed friend-ships with others who could sew. If I needed shoes for cheerleading, more babysitting was required. Our simple life was lush—new friends and better living conditions—and we all took it with acceptance and a "do your best" attitude. Mother called me her "sunshine" and my first night in my own bedroom I almost cried, feeling like a princess.

I had to, eventually, realize that being too talkative, or laughing when I was feeling stressed, wasn't appropriate. It was the 60s and I was a teen, but ready to move to an even larger town to find freedom in fully expressing myself. I continued to crave more experiences and see more of the world than this town on the expressway. College would offer that as well as friends of different backgrounds who would remain allies for life. My husband would be of a different background and, as the movie *Annie Hall* indicated, merging quiet families with argumentative ones would be a lifetime journey. Thus began the strong belief that people come into our lives to teach us our strengths.

Psychology 101 began with why we do what we do, and I was hooked in a story of myself and all the people around me. I had an insatiable appetite for Carl Jung, what my dreams were telling me that I wasn't recognizing in my awake state, and Joseph Campbell and the idea that we all had a Hero's Journey. Probably even more inspiring at my core was his quote, "We must be willing to let go of the life we planned so as to have the life that is waiting for us." The piano had always been a place of solitude, and without realizing it, I had worked out problems after being with the music. It soothed my soul. I had found music therapy before I knew what it was, and probably developed some of my ability to allow life to happen, while learning causes and effects along the way. A human resources career met my needs of helping others in Atlanta—a city where I could have close friends, but everyone didn't know everyone quite so intimately. Specializing in benefits, I became the confidant of other employees who needed help in insurance claims, including those with emotional and abusive issues. Soon, their diagnoses were changing and addictions and traumas of all types were given new treatment options and I found myself listening to their stories. I felt I made an impact, presenting a friendly face, and I found joy in the work. I also had to face my arch nemeses—anger and people who were suffering and sometimes showed their displeasure. But I was in a safe place with people who were working with professionals for their improvement. I had everything except balance as my work hours neared 80 each week. The meaningful questions of "Who am I?" "What do I want?" "What's my purpose in Life?" were yet unmined.

After 15 years of fertility tests, procedures, and lost applications in the state's system for adoptions, I held my new calling—a five-week-old son. Our prayers had been answered. I tried to juggle all the demands, but the career I had created wasn't adapting, and my Type A personality wasn't reassuring for this sweet new life that got cranky if he sensed my stress. My two former sidekicks, perfectionism and people-pleasing, were no longer needed or wanted. Reading all the baby books wasn't helping me achieve what his soul wanted—me to be present. He became my greatest teacher. I became lost in play, those genuine, life-altering moments of sheer bliss. Playing with animals, releasing butterflies, embracing Elmo at a musical, attending symphonies—all of these brought tears of joy as if heaven and earth had collided. Then, without warning, one day I said something that was all too familiar: "Please don't whine." I'd taken a version of my childhood and put it on him. I wasn't validating his emotions or trying to help him figure out how to speak what he was feeling. I was the adult, but I wasn't acting like one. We had utilized "Time Out" tactics (gems for both of us), but I hadn't thought of discussing agitation or annoyance or ways to handle them. We had run and twirled and done the physical outpouring of avoiding blow-ups, but I hadn't come to terms with my own triggers—the baggage from childhood. My own avoidance. I hadn't realized I was continuing to run from conflicts and angry dialogue. I wished for a harmonious world for us to grow into, but I hadn't been willing to even look at the not-so-cheerful side of life. I also needed to deal with those days when I wasn't "Little Miss Sunshine" myself.

To see the lessons our children have brought us is to lessen our ego, accept that every experience is a learning opportunity, and take nothing personally. I began journaling and found those internal dialogues needed expressing to see the light of day. Tiny fears or worries were signs that I was moving out of my comfort zone—a situation neither good nor bad, but something to embrace. The Zen philosophy of no judgment, no expectation, and giving up the need to know what's tomorrow (becoming detached from the outcome), continues to be an ideal for me.

I believe we're all born self-aware. What a blessing to remain that way throughout one's lifetime. I had, obviously, numbed some emotions through various activities and techniques. But once the forensics were in and I awakened to the possibility that I might need to face some fears, the answers, the teachers, and Divine Guidance continued to appear. I have moved from a faith in God to completely TRUSTING God. I was given tools to grow myself into a healthy human being and, for that and all the blessings I've been given, gratitude begins each day. Without the innate happiness bestowed upon me at birth, those sad moments or days could have been devastating. Without resilience, I wouldn't have been ready to tackle all the inner work that was needed.

It's no coincidence that Tolle's book *Being in the Now* became a new source of awareness for me, along with studying the Enneagram on all the personalities and the shadow sides of each. I recognized that when we heal ourselves—just by the higher vibration we put out—we heal those around us. Seeking out safe places and safe people to share the darkest thoughts, answers were just below the surface, awaiting the quiet to unfold.

As I learned more of the "whys" about myself, I was developing a new level of compassion and readying for forgiving others. Not only would there be a need to excise the old wounds, but I was reliving the original pain in order to reimagine my relationship to it, to the people, and to the possibility that my dad may have had more issues (including mental health challenges) than were addressed at that time. Perhaps, had he been given a healthy way to process emotions—including anger—he would have known better and acted kinder. I needed to know this, for my own peace of mind, since Mother had said she doesn't get angry. I felt when I lost my cool that I wasn't handling life as well as I should. It's all contracted energy and will only decrease the ability of expanding our awareness and our healing abilities for ourselves and others.

I began reading the book *Women Who Run With the Wolves* by Clarissa Pinkola Estes, PhD, and saw myself in some of the stories and archetypes. In time, I came to terms with the fact that if I have the intention of evolving and not being destructive, then healthy righteous indignation, justifiable anger, resentment, guilt, shame, retribution, etc. should be honored as transformational, which rids it from the body.

I sought out various healing modalities as I tried to give myself permission to fully and freely emote, to feel, and to speak when under stress. In the past, if anyone had a major argument, I would leave the area, seeking a safe refuge. If someone yelled at me, my throat would physically lock. I truly could not elicit a sound. Often I would leave and would not have a thoughtful response until the following day. Of course, walking away from someone slinging jarring and antagonizing words made me appear passive aggressive, and only later could I say in the best way I could (even in a shaky voice), "I need time and I'll talk later" prior to leaving a space that didn't seem emotionally or physically safe.

Learning to do the work of mediations—within the field of alternative dispute resolutions—helped me heal my childhood. I feel that mediations hold the key to resolving problems while lending your own voice to the outcome. It's empowerment of one's self—not the judges or the juries. At the same time, I continued the inner work and began remembering condescending phrases: "Are you giving me the silent treatment again?" "Are you still pouting?" And I rehearsed the answer: "I am still hurting. I need time and space." It's not perfect (I dropped that notion years ago), but I am honoring my voice, and I stand in this place, firmly and strongly, as the facilitator in resolving a dispute.

All through history, when humans participate in ceremony, they enter a "sacred space." I believe it is our duty on this earth, for our fellow humans, to hold a space for each other so they feel heard, validated, worthy. It's not always "right or wrong," because we all are consciously shaped by our filters, belief systems, and experiences. But as a mediator, I have hope that there is the possibility of finding common ground and possibly even shifting some perceptions. That's why I consider this my late-in-life calling: To give people a safe place to speak. I want to allow individuals a safe place to breathe deeply, to recollect the scattered parts of themselves, to regain mindfulness, and to speak in a sacred space. And I will listen, without judgment and without an agenda of how to fix it. For I believe that deep within, we each have the answers, if we can just find a safe and quiet place for the inquiry. I am no longer running from my childhood. It has given me more blessings than I would have imagined. I am going towards a fuller future, where listening is welcomed, smiles are appreciated, and a mindful voice is a Divine gift.

## Discussion Questions

1. When have you restricted your thoughts and opinions? How did that affect you? What did you feel?

2. Where do you feel safe? Where are you the most alive and authentic? What are you doing, saying, feeling? How can you bring those positive vibrations into your life on a regular basis?

3. What experiences from your past are still not healed? How can you honor the voice within? What everyday practice helps you grow your voice and become more yourself?

*Linda Goodman takes her experience as a mediator and helps individuals find their voice prior to attending a session. She also helps persons who have been involved in a challenging outcome or life situation become unstuck utilizing the tools she's learned for transformation. www.PeacefulResolutionsLLC.com*

# Afterword

Do you listen to your intuition? Are you aware of those inner nudges that help direct you on your path?

Long ago I received one of those nudges—a divine whisper—that gave me the title of *F.A.I.T.H.* – *Finding Answers in the Heart.* I loved the title and didn't know what to do with it, so I ignored the nudge. But it persisted. Time and again I heard the whisper and time and again I looked the other way. Until it became too loud to ignore. It took me over five years to create something from that title. But from that divine whisper came *F.A.I.T.H.*, a collection of extraordinary stories from ordinary women. Stories about marriage, finances, agoraphobia, and sexual abuse. Circumstances that challenged fourteen women to stand strong and resolute.

Creating the first volume of *F.A.I.T.H.* led me through the land of Uncertainty, with Doubt, Worry, and Fear lurking around every corner, always ready to hinder and obstruct. My story "Trust Me!" tells of the path that soared and plunged and almost derailed, but in the end Trust emerged victorious and the book was born.

When more women wanted to share their experiences, Volume II came to life, a second collection about love, surrender, forgiveness, and death. Heart-warming and heart-wrenching, these tales portray women from all walks of life who have stumbled and fallen and picked themselves up. As in the first book, the road for these women was not paved with gold or smooth asphalt or even soft grass. The situations they experienced were often unexpected and horrendous. But they found their way to their hearts' desire—through faith.

Faith is not a question of attitude. Faith is a deep inner knowing. A certainty. Trusting that life will be for the better, no matter what. It is expecting the best from every circumstance and responding to reality with a glass-half-full positivity. It is Pollyanna in the worst of times and glorious miracles all around you when you look for them.

One of the things I've learned this last year is to stop concentrating on what's wrong (not at all an easy task) and focus on what's right. There are so many times I'm envious of what other people do or have—festive celebrations, new clients, 7-figure incomes, trips around the world. I say the right words but my heart's not in them and, therefore, neither is my vibration. It's perfectly okay to want those things.

But when I come from a place of envy I tell the universe that I don't deserve them. When I can come from a place of abundance, then the well-wishing serves a purpose. I open myself to receiving and the universe happily complies. So instead of saying "How come she has that?" I can be truly happy for my friend or acquaintance and say "I want some of that too!"

To get in that mode, cultivate appreciation. Appreciation acts like a magnet. The more you appreciate what you have, the more you have to appreciate. When you're thankful for everything in your life—even the aches and pains, the loss of a job, a relationship breakup, and, yes, the death of a loved one—then life stops being a chore and starts being a miracle.

My life is now a series of miracles. Through the process of publishing *F.A.I.T.H.* I collaborated with 13 wonderful women to produce Volume I. Then 13 amazing women collaborated with me to complete Volume II. These women have enriched my life beyond bounds, offering their partnership, their friendship, and their unbelievable energy. Without them there would be no books, no community, and no fulfilling the vision to help others. *F.A.I.T.H.* has allowed these women to become authors, to be empowered as they broaden their horizons and their reality. By sharing their stories and passions with others, they reached for the stars and realized their dreams. And in writing their stories they touched other mothers, daughters, granddaughters, friends, business acquaintances. Women in their local communities, their states, across the country, and around the world. Women who have been inspired to heal, grow, and expand.

Are you a woman in need? Are you ready for miracles in your life? Your heart knows the way. That gut feeling, the voice in your head, that unexplainable sensation you have—those nudges are your guidance system. The more you pay attention to them, the better life will be.

It may not be easy. It may not happen overnight. But if you're willing to start examining your life, you *can* make a change. The authors in Volumes I and II found their way.

We invite you to join us. It's your time now. All it takes is a little *F.A.I.T.H.—Finding Answers in the Heart.*

# About the Authors

# Azizi Blissett

Azizi Blissett is an accomplished artist and inspirational leader with a purpose and passion for encouraging others to tap into their creative selves to live an authentic life.

She discovered her unique voice and soul's purpose through art and creative expression, which became a form of self-empowerment and emotional independence that transformed her negative beliefs and life experiences to build a self-sufficient and independent life.

A "unique and rare" individual as her Swahili name suggests, Azizi is an innovative change agent who inspires women and youth to listen to their inner guidance, embrace their true power, and live a fulfilling life.

A native of St. Louis, Azizi is the daughter of two talented artists. Her creative passion stems from early childhood, listening to her parent's band perform original reggae music and rhythms throughout various local and international venues. She is the product of their creativity, entrepreneurial spirit, and community-mindedness.

After a successful career in corporate America, Azizi made a challenging decision to switch careers from business marketing at a leading computer company to pursue a career in Advertising. During Fall 2007, she took her next courageous leap into entrepreneurship as she launched her own marketing company and non-profit organization. Azizi has transformed her former marketing business to her dynamic personal brand, AziziBlissett.com, which includes her Life Coaching, Brand Marketing, and Creative Direction/TV Production services. Her personal art collage series, The Redefinition of Me, is available at http://www.cafepress.com/theredefinitionofmeartcollection.

info@zfusion.org
www.zfusion.org
Facebook – www.facebook.com/zfusioninc

# Terry Crump

Terry Crump, PhD, is a licensed clinical psychologist who is passionate about holistic health and whose purpose is to contribute to others' healing and wellness. She is the owner of Crump Wellness Services where psychological and stress management services are offered. Dr. Terry has served as an adjunct professor who thoroughly enjoys teaching about human growth and development, mental health/illness, cultural sensitivity, and racial/ethnic disparities in healthcare. She has given workshops on psychological testing and stress management, and has coauthored a chapter in pediatric psychology on Family Systems and Health. Initially trained to work primarily with children and families, Dr. Terry maintains her commitment to youth through board membership and volunteer work with a nonprofit organization providing mentorship programming in Atlanta.

In her spare time, Dr. Terry is an avid supporter of the visual and performing arts, attending plays, concerts, and exhibits whenever the opportunity arises. As well, she maintains close ties with family and friends. Dr. Terry aspires to write children's and nonfiction books in the near future.

drterry@crumpwellness.com
www.crumpwellness.com
Facebook – www.facebook.com/crumpwellness
LinkedIn – www.linkedin.com/in/drcrump

# Linda Goodman

Linda Goodman makes her home in Atlanta, Georgia where she is a Reiki Master, Mediator, and Consultant/Coach. She credits the mediation tool of being "neutral" as one of the foundations for bringing beneficial healing to others by an almost sacred listening technique and allowing others to experience their own deeply personal answers in a safe environment.

After a career in Human Resources and working within companies to show them how to work generationally and develop teams for their benefit , Linda decided to go one-on-one to allow for more personal transformation of her clients. Her desire is to continue to morph her business based on the needs of her clients. Several have requested assistance on teaching their children to effectively emote, and a collaborative project is currently being developed for that purpose.

Aristotle's "Know Better, Do Better" is Linda's motto in helping others as well as herself. In that vein, she continues to study The Enneagram and the healthy vs. shadow sides of each personality. She's involved in the Jung Society and is passionate in her study of Kabbalah with a Rabbi. In Linda's words, "studying from the source resonates on a soul level."

Classical Music and Italian Operas resound from her vehicle and home, shared by dogs and her husband. She's proud of the accomplishments of her dear family members, especially her adult son. They often humor her by attending positive thinking seminars or guided meditations, which makes her smile even broader.

linda.goodman@mac.com
www.PeacefulResolutionsLLC.com

# Suzanne Baker Hogan

Suzanne Baker Hogan is a spiritual writer. She is a communicator of spiritual beauty, creativity, and meaning.

Suzanne grew up in a family of artists and earned a BA in philosophy from St. John's College in Annapolis, Maryland and Santa Fe, New Mexico. She went on to work in international business and translation, helping clients to communicate all over the world in dozens of languages. Suzanne then followed her passion to become a full-time professional artist.

For ten years, Suzanne enjoyed representation by Trinity Gallery, now Alan Avery Art, in Atlanta, Georgia. Working with wall-sized canvases, she explored metaphysical themes, painted souls of light, and memorialized the beauty of nature through poetry. Suzanne became a mother and continued to grow spiritually.

As her awakening accelerated, Suzanne began writing about her experiences and found her highest purpose. She is here to remind you of the inner beauty, creativity, and meaning that have always been an integral part of you. Suzanne wants to help you actualize your fullest human potential during these extraordinary times. She is the author of *Share the Spiritual*, a metaphysical blog, and is currently working on several books. Suzanne has begun the blog *Twin Flame Help* to assist others going through a Twin Flame experience.

678.613.3720
suzart444@icloud.com
www.sharethespiritual.com
Blog – www.twinflamehelp.wordpress.com

# About the Authors

# Barbara J. Hopkinson

Barbara J. Hopkinson helps families struggling with grief after the loss of a child to find hope and happiness again. Following her adult son's sudden death in a motorcycle accident (and the loss of two infants before that), Barbara founded a local chapter, The Compassionate Friends of Greater Newburyport, part of an international organization. She is a model of hope, having helped hundreds of families.

Her unique perspective of personal loss and intimately witnessing so many bereaved families in grief formed the basis of her first book *A Butterfly's Journey . . . Healing Grief After the Loss of a Child*. The book, along with her local retreats, online Resource Center, and individualized virtual options expand her support for bereaved families.

She received acknowledgment from New York Times' bestselling author Andre Dubus, who declared *her book* to be "an important and timely contribution to the literature of spiritual and life-loving resilience." Barbara interviewed on several TV shows and radio stations. Visit www.abutterflysjourney.com for podcasts, videos, helpful blog topics, and other resources.

Barbara lives north of Boston with her husband, Jim. She enjoyed a successful career in international technology, including ten years as an IBM executive. Barbara has great relationships with her son, Brad, and three adult stepchildren, Melanie, Matthew, and Christopher. She also has a passion for cooking, photography, and travel, having visited forty-six countries so far.

617.410.6309
barbara@abutterflysjourney.com
www.abutterflysjourney.com
Facebook – www.facebook.com/abutterflysjourney
Twitter – www.twitter.com/AButterflysJour

# Judy Keating, MA

Judy has discovered that her God-given gifts and talents are in her ability to be with people. People who are grieving, people in transition, or people who are interested in transformation are drawn to her work. Judy came to understand that having a loving, compassionate, and grateful relationship with herself was her life's work. Sharing that journey with others has led to her becoming an author, speaker, facilitator, and energy conduit. She works with individuals as well as small and large groups to bring a grounded perspective that alleviates suffering and rejuvenates others' life purpose.

Judy utilized her own journey of recovering from extreme self-doubt and debilitating self-judgment to explore and learn healing modalities, sacred practices, and deep listening so that she could have joy, peace, and a deeper connection to Source. She has termed her work Inner Life Coaching as all of her offerings help people find peace and ease within themselves.

Judy is an advanced Crystalline Consciousness Technique™ practitioner, a Usui and Karuna Reiki Master, and is certified as a Creation coach, facilitator, and author through the Natural Rhythms Institute. She has trained with Lisa Michaels; Martha Beck, PhD; Michael Trotta; Melani Marx; and Martha Atkins, PhD. Judy has learned from a lifelong physical disability the vital human need to laugh about our own fallible mischief. She has assisted both groups and individuals to recognize what's right in their lives for over twenty years. She lives with her husband in a suburb of Atlanta, Georgia.

judy@innerlifecoaching.net
www.innerlifecoaching.net
Facebook – www.facebook.com/judy.keating.50

# Rebecca Kirson

Rebecca Kirson is a transformational coach for life and business, Akashic Record Practitioner, and inspirational speaker who is committed to raising her clients' levels of awareness so they can live in alignment with their Soul's Purpose and authentic truth. A life of fulfillment doesn't just happen to us; we create it with conscious awareness, a defined vision, and commitment towards our life design.

Rebecca works with clients to give them the intuitive wisdom and soul-level healing from the Akashic Records in conjunction with loving guidance and support as they begin to shift the areas of their lives where they are playing small and hiding their light. Rebecca has an Executive MBA, plus a background in Psychology, Human Development, and Family Studies. She is also a certified Soul Realignment Practitioner™ and Soul Realignment Practitioner for Business and Financial Abundance™. Her wisdom encompasses expanding one's consciousness, the dynamics and effect of family and relationships, and navigating the journey of Entrepreneurship.

Rebecca's business, Your Sacred Truth, embraces the mission to "Expand Awareness for the Journey of Your Soul." Rebecca works with clients via Akashic Record Readings, individual coaching sessions, inspirational classes, and workshops, and she has a monthly show on the Wisdom and Intuition Network (WIN) which airs the third Thursday of the month. You can learn more about this monthly program at www.metaphysicalwisdom.com.

Rebecca resides in Atlanta, Georgia with her husband Joel and her animal companions.

rebecca@yoursacredtruth.com
www.yoursacredtruth.com
Facebook – www.facebook.com/yoursacredwisdom
Twitter – www.twitter.com/yoursacredtruth

# Nanette
# Littlestone

Nanette Littlestone loves playing with words, Roget's Thesaurus, and word puzzles. Writing that flows is thrilling. Writer's block is not. She's also intuitive, heart-centered, slightly irreverent, and has a wacky sense of humor which she offsets with a generous smile.

Nanette is a writing coach, editor, author, publisher, and CEO of Words of Passion. She helps inspirational authors overcome writer's block, master correct grammar, create strong structure, and write with clarity and passion by blending the technicalities of writing with intuition, emotion, and heart. Over twenty years of experience with both fiction and nonfiction (plus advanced degrees in Resistance, Doubt, and Worry) kindle Nanette's passion for assisting authors to achieve their own unique message. She specializes in helping women write from the heart so they can put their passion into words and inspire others. Finding that place of struggle within her clients and unlocking the door to create change and opportunity is what makes her heart soar.

On the publishing side, Nanette believes that becoming an author doesn't have to be difficult. She created the Partner Up! Book Program to help women entrepreneurs get published the easy way through collaborative books. She is the editor and coauthor of *The 28-Day Thought Diet*, editor and coauthor of *F.A.I.T.H. – Finding Answers in the Heart, Volumes I and II*, and author of the forthcoming book *Overcoming Writer's Block: Moving from Fear to Passion*. Her coaching programs and services offer clients unique and in-depth ways to strengthen their manuscripts and make their writing sing.

nanette@wordsofpassion.com
www.wordsofpassion.com
Facebook – www.facebook.com/wordsofpassion
LinkedIn – www.linkedin.com/in/wordsofpassion

# Ricia L. Maxie

An internationally renowned intuitive consultant/mystic, Reiki practitioner, and speaker, Ricia loves to help people with her God-given ability. She uses prayer and meditation to deepen her readings and connect with spirit guides, angels, and those who have passed beyond this physical dimension.

Born with intuitive gifts that continued to expand through the years, Ricia received training from a variety of teachers and guides in body and not in body. She uses a range of skills, combined with her gifts, which include clairvoyance, clairaudience, claircognizance, clairsentience, mediumship, and channeling.

For thirty years, Ricia has been helping people find the answers they need. Services include intuitive consultations, spiritual and intuitive development classes, workshops, retreats, guided meditation, past life regressions, hypnosis, Reiki, and personal growth coaching.

Ricia L. Maxie is also a change management and organization development consultant who is an experienced facilitator, coach, and instructor. She teaches communication and collaboration at all levels of an organization and facilitates team building, interest-based problem solving, and conflict resolution. She has coached executives and employees on leadership techniques and effective communication, which results in increased morale. Processes for organization-wide change initiatives or simply department level accord have been her specialty.

Ricia earned a BA in psychology from Dominican University and an MA in counseling psychology from the University of San Francisco.

707.280.2404 (Can receive calls or text)
ricialm@aol.com
www.RiciaLMaxie.com
Facebook – www.facebook.com/RicialmaxieIntuitive

# Corinna Murray

Corinna Murray, DVM, CPC is a veterinarian, iPEC Certified Professional Coach, and founder of EnHABiT™ (Engaging the Human Animal Bond in Tandem) and Veterinary Care Navigation™. Corinna brings years of experience as a practicing veterinarian to these unique services focused on enhancing the quality of the bonds that people have with their pets. Her experiential approach in teaching people emotional management, in order to get the behaviors and bonds they are looking for, is simple, effective, and enjoyable for everyone involved. Corinna also provides counsel on reconciling difficult situations and decision making.

Framed by a core belief that all of nature is purposefully interconnected, Corinna is a perpetual student of the natural world. Her interests grow from her insatiable curiosity and empathic tendencies. Corinna's love for and connections with animals led to her successful career in Veterinary Medicine. Her love for people and personal development led her later in life to coaching. Corinna also enjoys being a certified yoga instructor, author, speaker, workshop facilitator, and volunteer for several animal welfare and service organizations and studies animal communication. She combines all her skills to empower others to achieve sustainable emotional satisfaction and to become the stress-free people they (and their pets) have always wanted.

Corinna lives in Johns Creek, Georgia with her husband and best friend, Mike, her less-abled daughter, Cally, Wookie (Cally's service dog), and kitties Sadie and Buster. Her grown sons, Jason and Kyle, enjoy living nearby in Atlanta.

404-661-2263
cm@drcorinnamurray.com
www.drcorinnamurray.com
LinkedIn – www.linkedin.com/in/drcorinnamurray

# Lynn Rekvig

With over 25 years as a registered nurse caring for patients and managing health care providers, Lynn has had the opportunity to meet and work with many talented individuals. A bachelor's degree in Nursing and a Master of Business Administration degree in Executive Management helped Lynn learn a lot about managing people and analyzing problems with a left brain linear approach.

A few years ago, Lynn won an Internet contest to work privately with a coach named Carol Look and was introduced to Emotional Freedom Technique (also known as EFT or tapping). EFT acts like a combination of acupressure and psychology that can create significant changes in relatively short periods of time. Through this unique opportunity, a new world opened up for Lynn in terms of approaching life issues and problems from an entirely new perspective.

Thanks to working in collaboration with Carol Look as one of her seven top coaches in the world, Lynn has been training others to become coaches using EFT. She specializes in helping people get unstuck by showing them how to remove barriers that hold them back from achieving their goals. Her intuitive depth and heart-centered compassion create a safe space for others to experience personal growth and transformation.

LRekvig@gmail.com
OptimalOutcomesRx.com
LinkedIn – www.LinkedIn.com/pub/Lynn-Rekvig

# Lorelei Robbins

Lorelei believes that each of us has a song to sing and that no one will die on her watch with their music in them. *Singing your song* is about being who you really are inside and out. It's about giving every single part of you a voice. Lorelei helps people realize their dreams by having the courage to DARE to dream, to RELEASE what's in the way, and to SURRENDER to Divine timing.

Using the power of the Lunar cycles and other planetary energies, Lorelei guides people to accelerate their dreams and manifest their heart's desires in perfect timing. She sees the light and the beauty in others and reflects it back to them. Once the light is turned on inside, anything is possible. Her unique skills as a spiritual astrologer, counselor, interviewer, and ordained minister are all in service to the manifestation of dreams.

Lorelei has a great passion for relationships and believes that *Every Match Is Made in Heaven*, because every relationship is a *holy encounter* that provides us with a mirror image of ourselves. She has inspired thousands of individuals to enhance the quality of their relationships by knowing that we *script* and *attract* everyone into our lives for a reason. And only we can change the script.

For seven years Lorelei was featured on Atlanta radio station B 98.5FM as their *Relationship Astrologer*. Twenty years of successful personnel consulting has positioned her as a leading advisor for progressive businesses.

404.226.0902
Loreleiyes@aol.com
www.robbinscosmicnest.com
Facebook – www.facebook.com/lorelei.robbins.7

# Angela Rodriguez

Angela Rodriguez is currently a Sergeant of Police for the San Francisco Police Department. Being a native of San Francisco, she is proud to be in service to the citizens of San Francisco, and has done so since 1999.

Though she has had various assignments in her career, she has most enjoyed working with children as a School Resource Officer and encouraging young adults to "keep their eyes on the prize" and to "dream big."

A dedicated supporter of those in need, Angela loves to volunteer her time in support of Make-A-Wish® Foundation, Special Olympics, and any and all programs surrounding children, the elderly, and animals.

Choosing a career in law enforcement was an obvious path for Angela as she realized that while searching for her "life's gift," it was revealed that truly listening with a compassionate heart was indeed her gift.

To balance and understand the different energies she encounters while in uniform, Angela studies and practices the philosophies of Science of Mind and is also an Advanced Reiki Practitioner.

Upon retirement, Angela intends to purchase a home in Sedona, Arizona in Boynton Canyon, where she plans to write two books.

# Maureen Roe

Maureen is a dedicated self-esteem coach who helps people overcome limiting beliefs, negative mindsets, self-criticism and judgment, and feelings of unworthiness. She's spent much of her career helping people shift their personal beliefs to think differently and feel better about themselves. Whether it's past experiences, fear of not being accepted, or just never feeling "good enough," she guides her clients to ease the judgment and feel worthy to be the best selves they can be.

Coming from an authoritative and critical environment, Maureen experienced her own limitations in being able to authentically express herself in both her personal life and her business career, which limited her achievements and success. Her own personal journey and extensive career experience produces one recurring theme: her dedication to nurturing people through coaching support and spiritual guidance in their authentic personal expression and worthiness.

Maureen is a master builder of the practical aspects of life. With her natural talent to bring order to chaos, she helps clients build stable foundations using wisdom teachings and positive psychology. Whether faced with a negative orientation, a life circumstance change, or aging issues, Maureen helps her clients create a solid platform from which to have a more practical belief in themselves and to launch a new outlook on life and express their authenticity.

In addition to her Master's of Science in Administration, Maureen is also a Registered Corporate Coach, an Ageless Grace instructor, and an ordained metaphysical minister. For more information please visit her website at www.maureenroecoaching.com, or call her at 404-293-0614.

404.293.0614
www.maureenroecoaching.com

# Share Your Story

Do you have a personal story of triumph to share? If you're like the women in this book who have overcome challenges in their lives through perseverance, determination, and faith, then we invite you to participate in the Third Volume of *F.A.I.T.H.* Millions of people around the world deserve to be healthier, stronger, more courageous, following their passions. Help us to help them by sharing inspiration.

Please visit www.FindingAnswersInTheHeart.com/participation for more information.

Thank you for reading *F.A.I.T.H.*

We encourage you to connect with the authors
using the contact information listed on their bios.

If you'd like more F.A.I.T.H.,
please sign up for the newsletter at
www.FindingAnswersInTheHeart.com

Share your comments about F.A.I.T.H.
by emailing comments@FindingAnswersInTheHeart.com